Bangkok

Front cover: Monks at Wat
Phra Kaew
Right: Wat Phra Kaew's
gilded stupa

TOP 10 ATTRACTIONS

Grand Palace and Wat Phra Kaew. These buildings represent some of the city's oldest and most beautiful architecture. See page 27.

Wat Traimit. The temple houses a 5.5-tonne solid gold Buddha. See page 40.

Royal Barges National Museum. Offers a glimpse into a water-borne world of ceremony and pageantry. See page 44.

Khao San Road. Asia's biggest and most popular backpacking hub. See page 54.

Vimanmek Mansion. Built from teak, it is a splendid example of Bangkok's Victorian-meets-Thai architecture. See page 57.

Wat Pho. Bangkok's oldest temple contains the longest reclining Buddha in Thailand. See page 31.

Jim Thompson's House. Visit the famous expat's house, full of beautiful art and antiques. See page 61.

Erawan Shrine. Traditional spirit worship and Hinduism combine here. See page 65.

Thonburi. Colourful longtail boats ply its network of canals, offering another perspective on the city. See page 43.

National Museum. Every period of Thai history is displayed and documented in its stately buildings. See page 35.

A PERFECT DAY

8.30am Breakfast

Get an early start and a river breeze to beat the heat with breakfast on the terrace of the Mandarin Oriental. It is rich with history, as Bangkok's most famous hotel, and the boats lend a relaxing backdrop.

9.30am Chinatown

A 15-minute taxi ride and you're at Wat Mangkon Kamalawat, Chinatown's biggest and most important temple. Later, wander down the evocative Soi Itsaranupap, a historic lane packed with Chinese culture, traditional streetfood and a 200 year-old market.

11.30am Art shows

Next take a taxi to the Bangkok Art & Culture Centre, which has temporary exhibitions of local and international works displayed over several floors. The gallery often features Thailand's best established and rising stars.

12.30pm Siam Square

The Siam Square zone marks the beginning of Bangkok's downtown shopping malls, so there's lots of choice when it comes to lunch. A good option is the ground floor food court at Siam Paragon mall for a range of local streetfood, reasonably priced and in air-conditioned comfort.

1.30pm Ocean World

In the basement of Siam Paragon is Ocean World, which has tanks containing some 30,000 marine species. You can take a glass-bottomed boat ride, go diving with sharks and marvel at South African penguins.

IN BANGKOK

4.00pm — Time for pampering

After a long day, there's nothing better than a relaxing massage, and Bangkok is full of pampering options. The nearby Grand Hyatt Erawan hotel has a luxury rooftop day spa, while Siam Square has many streetside parlours to ease those aching limbs.

9.00pm — Nightlife

Still at the bottom end of Silom Road, Maggie Choo's is one of the city's classiest and most imaginative nightlife spots. It's based on a vision of slinky 1930s' Shanghai, with a slightly naughty vibe, great sounds and serious drinks. They also have a period-style noodle shop, so you could just as easily eat here.

2.30pm — Shopping

Paragon is just one of many malls along this stretch, with a phenomenal choice, whether you want high fashion, smartphones, spices, or copies of master artworks executed by painters in MBK. You can use skywalks between several of the malls, so you avoid the cluttered pavements below.

5.30pm — Sunset cocktails

A taxi to the bottom of Silom Road brings you to Sirocco, a 300-metre-high rooftop restaurant and bar that provides a stunning view for sunset cocktails. Either linger here for dinner or take a five-minute walk around the corner for a choice of Thai at Harmonique.

CONTENTS

INTRODUCTION

Bangkok is one of the most exciting and dynamic cities in Southeast Asia. Double-digit economic growth during the 1980s and 1990s brought air-conditioned shopping malls, elevated and underground urban railways and world-class architectural experiments. A severe recession in the late 1990s nearly halted the economy but prompted an inwardly focused artistic renaissance that included critically hailed Thai new-wave cinema and an explosion of independent music. Recent years have seen renewed economic buoyancy, and the rapid building of new condos, offices and hotels, but also social unrest and mass demonstrations. Despite these troubles Bangkok continues to lure curious visitors from around the world with its unique blend of the spiritual, carnal and entrepreneurial.

A distinctive capital

Straddling the Chao Phraya River delta, metropolitan Bangkok covers 1,569 sq km (606 sq miles) and sprawls into the neighbouring provinces of Nonthaburi, Samut Prakan and Samut Sakhon. The rivers and tributaries of northern and central Thailand drain into the Chao Phraya River, which in turn disgorges into the Gulf of Thailand, a vast cul-de-sac of the South China Sea only a few kilometres from central Bangkok.

The capital is surrounded on three sides by a huge, wet, flat and extremely fertile area known as 'the rice bowl of Asia' – more rice is grown here than in any other area of comparable size in all of Asia. Thailand has, in fact, been the world's top exporter of rice for at least the last 30 years. A vast spider web of natural and artificial canals fan out through this sultry river delta for several hundred square kilometres. Criss-crossing the

The skytrain passing through the city at night

city in all directions, these murky green waterways conjure up a parallel universe in which 18th-century Siam collides with 21st-century Thailand.

The capital is administered as a separate province, and has the only elected governorship in the nation (other provincial governors are appointed by the ministry). Press freedoms envied by neighbouring nations have made Bangkok Asia's largest base for foreign media correspondents. As a primary gateway for investment in neighbouring Vietnam, Cambodia, Laos and Myanmar, the city also serves as a financial hub for mainland Southeast Asia.

Banking, finance, wholesale and retail trade, transport, tourism and energy dominate the immediate municipality, while the surrounding metropolitan area adds manufacturing, shipping, food processing and intensive farming to the list of top revenue producers. Per capita income in metropolitan Bangkok runs well above the average in the rest of the country.

Figures on Bangkok's infamous nightlife-based economy are difficult to come by, and civic leaders prefer to keep it that way. When Longman's *Dictionary of Contemporary English* defined Bangkok as 'a place where there are a lot of prostitutes', Thais filed diplomatic protests and staged demonstrations outside the British Embassy. Longman agreed to withdraw the offending edition from circulation, although the blunder was echoed a few years later when Microsoft's *Encarta* labelled Bangkok as a 'commercial sex hub', resulting in a lawsuit and subsequent revision of the entry.

At the floating market

Population

Official estimates place metropolitan Bangkok's population at 8 million, though some claim this figure may be as much as 7 million short as the city has many unregistered residents. An astonishing 5,000 residents compete for every square kilometre, propelling a creative turbine that never ceases as the city's past and future co-evolve, from farms to freeways, spirit shrines to art galleries. Visitors won't be surprised to hear that one in eight Thais lives in Bangkok, or that 60 percent of the country's wealth is concentrated here.

Built-up Bangkok

Only a little over half of the city's inhabitants are ethnic Thais, with Thai as their first language. Although Thais are found in all walks of life, they are the backbone of Bangkok's blue-collar workforce, especially construction, automotive repair and river transport.

Up to 25 percent of the city's population is of Chinese or mixed Thai and Chinese descent. Many Bangkok Chinese-Thais speak both Thai and a Chinese dialect, such as Cantonese, Hokkien or Chiu Chau. Chinese influence is so strong that in certain areas of the city – such as Yaowarat, Bangkok's Chinatown, or Pathumwan, the city's wealthiest precinct – you can almost imagine you're in Hong Kong or Singapore rather than Thailand. In these areas Chinese tend to be engaged in all manner of commerce, from wholesale trade in auto parts

Buddhas in Wat Suthat

to the manufacture of high-end kitchen utensils. In other parts of the city they dominate higher education, international trade, banking and white-collar employment in general.

Bangkok's second-largest Asian minority claims South Asian descent, most tracing their heritage to northern India, including many Sikhs who immigrated during the 1947 Partition of India. Many of the city's South Asians can be found in a neighbourhood known as Phahurat (off the northern end of Yaowarat Road, between Chakraphet and Phahurat roads), or in Bangrak (along Charoen Krung Road, near junctions with Silom and Surawong roads). In both areas they operate a multitude of successful retail businesses, particularly textile and tailor shops.

People from the Middle East probably reached Thailand before most other ethnic groups, including the Thais themselves, having traded along the Thai coastlines in the early years of the first Christian millennium. The first global oil crisis in the 1970s saw a renewal of Arab business interests in Bangkok, and today the area known as Nana, roughly extending from Soi 3 to Soi 11 along Sukhumvit Road, sees a high concentration of both residents and tourists from the Middle East.

Bangkok's residents of European descent number around 45,000. The vast majority, unlike their Asian counterparts, find themselves in Thailand for only a few months or years for reasons of work or study. As a reflection of their countries' significant roles in the early development of Bangkok, residents of German and British descent appear to be most prominent.

Religion

Around 92 percent of Bangkokians follow Theravada Buddhism, the world's oldest and most traditional Buddhist sect. Walk the streets of Bangkok early in the morning and you'll catch rows of shaved heads bobbing above bright ochre robes, as monks all over the city engage in the daily house-to-house alms-food-gathering. Thai men are expected to don monastic robes temporarily at least once in their lives. Some enter the monkhood twice, first as 10-vow novices in their pre-teen years and then as fully ordained, 227-vow monks some time after the age of 20.

Thai Buddhists believe that individuals work out their own paths to *nibbana* (nirvana) through a combination of good works, meditation and study of the *dhamma* or Buddhist philosophy. The presence of *wats* (monasteries) scattered around the city serves as a reminder that Buddhism retains a certain dominance even in increasingly secular Bangkok.

Green-hued onion domes looming over rooftops belong to mosques and mark the immediate neighbourhood as Muslim, while brightly painted and ornately carved cement spires indicate a Hindu temple. Wander down congested Chakraphet Road in the Phahurat district to find Sri Gurusingh Sabha, a Sikh temple where visitors are welcome. A handful of steepled Christian churches, some

What's a wat?

Bangkok has over 300 Buddhist monasteries (*wat* in Thai), each consisting of a walled compound containing several buildings constructed in the traditional Thai style with steep, swooping rooflines and colourful interior murals.

Young novice monks

of them historic, have taken root over the centuries and can be found near the banks of the Chao Phraya River. In Chinatown large round doorways topped with heavily inscribed Chinese characters and flanked by red paper lanterns denote *san jao*, Chinese temples dedicated to the worship of Buddhist, Taoist and Confucian deities.

Something for everyone

As varied as it is vast, Bangkok offers residents and visitors alike the assurance they will never be bored. One can move across the city on water via 18th-century canals, in the air aboard the sleek Skytrain or below ground in the high-tech Metropolitan Rapid Transit Authority (mrta) subway. When hunger beckons, residents are spoiled by a panoply of the finest Thai restaurants anywhere in the kingdom, along with a host of other Asian cuisines and a broad range of European fare prepared by native chefs. Night falls and one can attend a classical Thai masked dance-drama performance followed by a club jaunt to hear a visiting DJ spin the latest house music. One of Asia's best-kept secrets when it comes to shopping, the city offers everything from custom-tailored suits to Asian antiques at prices no other Asian capital can rival.

Bangkok also serves as a convenient base for excursions to Nakhon Pathom (location of Thailand's largest Buddhist *stupa*, or monument), Kanchanaburi (Bridge on the River Kwai), Ayutthaya and the island of Ko Samet.

A BRIEF HISTORY

Founded barely 200 years ago, Bangkok can't claim an ancient pedigree. Yet its relatively brief history has seen the transformation of a small river-bank trading village into what is arguably Southeast Asia's most dynamic and colourful capital.

Bangkok's predecessor

Bangkok's political and cultural identity originally took shape 86km (53 miles) upriver in Ayutthaya, the royal capital of Siam – as Thailand was then known – from 1350 to 1767. Encircled by rivers with access to the Gulf of Thailand, Ayutthaya flourished as a sea port courted by Dutch, Portuguese, French, English, Chinese and Japanese merchants. By the end of the 17th century, Ayutthaya had a population of 1 million and was one of the wealthiest and most powerful cities in Asia.

Throughout four centuries of Ayutthaya reign, several European powers tried without success to establish colonial relationships with the kingdom of Siam. A Burmese army finally subdued the

Wat Rachaburana by night in the Historical Park, Ayuthaya

capital in 1767, destroying most of Ayutthaya's Buddhist temples and royal edifices.

Founding a new capital

Four years after this devastating defeat, the Siamese regrouped under Phaya Taksin, a half-Chinese, half-Thai general who decided to move the capital further south along the Chao Phraya River, closer to the Gulf of Siam. Thonburi Si Mahasamut, founded 200 years earlier by a group of wealthy Thais who had turned it into an important trade entrepôt during the height of Ayutthaya's power, was a logical choice.

Fearing Thailand was vulnerable to further Burmese attacks from the west, in 1782 Taksin's successor Phaya Chakri moved the capital across the river to a smaller settlement known as Bang Makok, after the *makok* (olive plum) trees which grew there in abundance. As the first monarch of the new Chakri royal dynasty – which continues to this day – Phaya Chakri was later dubbed King Rama I.

Under Rama I, the Siamese erected a new royal palace, raised 10km (6 miles) of city walls and dug a system of

River re-routing

One of the city's major physical transformations occurred in the late 18th century with the digging of a canal to create a short cut across a large bend in the Chao Phraya River, thus hastening water transport to the north.

The Chao Phraya's original river course along that bend gradually diverted much of its volume to the canal short cut. Today, most visitors and residents are unaware that the section of river running along the immediate west of Ko Rattanakosin is technically an artificial canal. Meanwhile, the original river loop, nowadays assumed to be a khlong (canal), has taken on the name of Khlong Bangkok Noi.

canals to create a moated, royal 'island' known as Ko Rattanakosin. Sections of the 4.5m (15ft) thick walls can still be seen near Wat Saket and the Golden Mount, and along the Chao Phraya River. The canal-moats still flow, albeit sluggishly, around the original royal district.

Early waterway map

Craftsmen who had survived the sacking of Ayutthaya built several magnificent temples and royal administrative buildings for the new capital. In 1785, the city was given a new name: *Krungthep mahanakhon bowon rattanakosin mahintara ayu-thaya mahadilok popnopparat ratchathani burirom udomratchaniwet mahasathan amonpima avatansathir sakkathatitya visnukamprasit*. The name translates as 'Great city of angels, the repository of divine gems, the great land unconquerable, the grand and prominent realm, the royal and delightful capital city full of nine noble gems, the highest royal dwelling and grand palace, the divine shelter and living place of reincarnated spirits'.

Foreign traders continued to call the capital Bang Makok, which eventually truncated itself to 'Bangkok', the name most commonly known to the outside world today. The Thais, meanwhile, commonly use a shortened version of the given name, Krung Thep (City of Angels).

Kings Rama II and Rama III ordered the building of more temples, and the system of rivers, streams and natural canals surrounding the capital was augmented by the excavation of additional waterways.

Trains go from the Dutch-designed Hualamphong
Railway Station

Water-borne traffic dominated the city, supplemented by
a meagre network of footpaths, well into the middle of the
19th century. In response to requests from diplomats and
international merchants, Rama IV (King Mongkut, 1851–68)
established a handful of roadways suitable for horse-drawn
carriages and rickshaws in the mid-1800s. The first – and most
ambitious road project for nearly a century to come – was
Charoen Krung Road (also known by its English name, New
Road), which ran 10km (6 miles) south from Wat Pho along
the east bank of the Chao Phraya River. This swathe of hand-
laid cobblestone, which took four years to finish, eventually
accommodated a tramway as well as early automobiles.

His successor Rama V (King Chulalongkorn, 1868–1910)
added the much wider Ratchadamnoen Klang Road to provide a suitably royal promenade – modelled after the Champs-
Elysées and lined with ornamental gardens – between the

Grand Palace and the expanding commercial centre to the east of Ko Rattanakosin.

Despite its modest size, the capital administered the much larger kingdom of Siam – which extended well into parts of what are today Laos, Cambodia and Malaysia – quite well. Even more impressive, Siamese rulers were able to stave off steady and occasionally intense pressure from the Portuguese, the Dutch, the French and the English, all of whom at one time or another wanted to add Siam to their colonial portfolios. By the end of the 19th century, France and England had established imperial rule in every one of Siam's neighbouring countries – the French in Indochina and the English in Burma and Malaya.

Revolution, coup and counter-coup

In 1924, a handful of Thai students in Paris formed a group that met to discuss ideas for a future Siamese government modelled on Western democracy. After finishing their studies and returning to Bangkok, three of these students – lawyer

International influence

Bangkok's ability to maintain Siam's independence meant that the kingdom was free to draw upon the talents of any architect or transport developer in the world, a freedom that helps explain the enormous variety – both planned and unplanned – in the capital today.

Germans were hired to design and build railways emanating from the capital, while the Dutch contributed Bangkok's central railway station, today considered a minor masterpiece of civic Art Deco. Americans established Siam's first printing press along with the kingdom's first newspaper in 1844. The first Thai-language newspaper, *Darunovadha*, came along in 1874, and by 1900 Bangkok had three daily English-language newspapers, the *Bangkok Times*, *Siam Observer* and *Siam Free Press*.

Royal Barges for Rama VII's coronation, 1925

Pridi Banomyong and military officers Phibul Songkhram and Prayoon Phamonmontri – organised an underground 'People's Party' dedicated to the overthrow of the Siamese system of government. The People's Party found a willing accomplice in Rama VII, and a bloodless revolution in 1932 transformed Thailand from an absolute monarchy into a constitutional one.

Phibul Songkhram, appointed prime minister by the People's Party in December 1938, changed the country's name from Siam to Thailand and introduced the Western solar calendar. When the Japanese invaded Southeast Asia in 1941, outflanking Allied troops in Malaya and Burma, Phibul allowed them access to the Gulf of Thailand. Japanese troops bombed and briefly occupied parts of Bangkok on their way to the Thai-Burmese border to fight the British in Burma and, as a result of public insecurity, the Thai economy stagnated.

Phibul resigned in 1944 under pressure from the Thai underground resistance, and after VJ Day in 1945 was exiled to

Japan. After three years, Phibul returned to Thailand and took over the leadership again via a military coup. Over the next 15 years, bridges were built over Mae Nam Chao Phraya, canals were filled in to provide space for new roads, and multi-storey buildings began crowding out traditional teak structures.

Another coup installed Field Marshal Sarit Thanarat in 1957, only to be deposed in 1964 by Thai army officers Thanom Kittikachorn and Praphat Charusathien, who ruled Thailand for nine years, allowing the US to establish several army bases within Thai borders to support the US campaign in Indochina. During this time Bangkok gained notoriety as a 'rest and recreation' (R&R) spot for foreign troops stationed in Southeast Asia.

In October 1973, the Thai military brutally suppressed a large pro-democracy student demonstration at Thammasat University in Bangkok, but King Bhumibol and General Krit Sivara, who sympathised with the students, refused to support further bloodshed, forcing Thanom and Praphat out. Oxford-educated leftist Kukrit Pramoj took charge of a 14-party coalition government and ejected the US military forces.

The Thai military regained control in 1976 after right-wing paramilitary groups assaulted a group of 2,000 students holding a sit-in at Thammasat, killing hundreds. Many students fled Bangkok and joined the People's Liberation Army of Thailand (PLAT), an armed Communist insurgency based in the hills since the 1930s.

Although a 1982 amnesty brought an end to PLAT, and students, workers and farmers returned to their homes, a new era of political tolerance exposed the military once again to civilian fire. In May 1992, several huge demonstrations demanding the resignation of the latest dictator, General Suchinda Kraprayoon, rocked Bangkok and the large provincial capitals. Bangkok governor Chamlong Srimuang, winner of the 1992 Magsaysay Award (a humanitarian service award issued in the Philippines) for his role in galvanising the public to reject

Suchinda, led the protests. After confrontations between the protesters and the military near the Democracy Monument resulted in nearly 50 deaths, King Bhumibol summoned both Suchinda and Chamlong for a rare public scolding. Suchinda resigned, having been in power for less than six weeks, and Chamlong's career was at an end.

As the 20th century roared across Asia, fuelled by a burst of prosperity and creativity Thailand had never seen before, Bangkok grew from a mere 13 sq km (5 sq miles) in 1900 to an astounding metropolitan area of over 330 sq km (127 sq miles) by the century's end. However, in 1997 the Thai currency fell into a deflationary tailspin and the national economy screeched to a virtual halt. Bangkok, which rode at the forefront of the 1980s double-digit economic boom, was more adversely affected than elsewhere in the country by job losses and massive income erosion.

People power has played a major role in recent Thai politics

Democratic struggles

In January 2001 after a land-slide election victory, bil-lionaire and former police colonel Thaksin Shinawatra was elected prime minister at the helm of a new party, Thai Rak Thai (TRT; Thai Love Thai). Thaksin's main sup-port was among Thailand's rural poor because he pro-posed increased funding for

Today Krung Thep Mahanak-hon embraces not only Bangkok proper, but also the former capital of Thonburi, across the Chao Phraya River to the west, along with the densely populated 'suburb' provinces of Samut Prakan to the east and Non-thaburi to the north.

health care and education. However, in the cities many quickly became disillusioned by its authoritarianism and corruption.

In 2005, anti-Thaksin demonstrators led by Chamlong Srimuang and media mogul Sondhi Limthongkul wore the colour yellow to show allegiance to the monarchy, becoming known as the Yellow Shirts. In January 2006 Thaksin enraged millions by selling his private telecom company Shin Corp to a Singapore firm without paying any tax, and in September a military junta overthrew the government while Thaksin was at a UN meeting in New York.

As Thaksin lived in exile, his followers, adopting red shirts, began their own protests. A Thaksin proxy, the People Power Party (PPP) won the next general election in December 2007. Thaksin returned the following year, but fled the country again after being found guilty of corruption.

The Yellow Shirts renewed demonstrations against the PPP government, laying siege to Government House and seizing Don Muang and Suvarnabhumi Airports, leaving thousands of holidaymakers stranded. The Constitutional Court ruled that the PPP should be disbanded for fraud.

The Oxford-educated leader of the Democrat Party Abhisit Vejjajiva formed a new coalition and became prime minister on 15 December 2008. The Red Shirts returned to the streets. Their disruption of the ASEAN summit held in Pattaya in April 2009 caused several heads of state to be airlifted to safety. In Bangkok, Yellow Shirt leader Sondhi was shot, but survived.

In February 2010, the courts found Thaksin guilty of abuse of power and confiscated B46 billion of his assets. Thousands of Red Shirts occupied parts of Bangkok in April and May, closing shopping malls. Eighty-five people were killed and nearly 1,500 injured in clashes with the army.

Another Thaksin proxy the Pheu Thai Party won a new election in 2011, and his sister Yingluck became Thailand's first female prime minister. Her government pushed for Constitutional change and a general amnesty for post-coup events. This was interpreted as an attempt to allow Thaksin to come home and regain his confiscated assets.

Late in 2013, yet another round of demonstrations closed major roads around the capital for several weeks. It led in early 2014 to a dissolved parliament and Pheu Thai being declared a caretaker government until new elections could be organised.

In May, the Constitutional Court removed Yingluck from office for abuse of power and she was indicted for dereliction of duty and negligence in the government's rice-pledging scheme, which was plagued with corruption. The army then staged another military coup. In August, the junta leader Prayuth Chan-ocha was named the new prime minister. Today, the situation remains fragile, not helped by the king's age causing uncertainty about the succession and attendant power structure.

Overburdened roads

Historical landmarks

1548 Ayutthaya merchants establish Thonburi Si Mahasamut on the banks of the Chao Phraya near the present site of Bangkok.

1767 Burmese armies sack Ayutthaya; Phaya Taksin declares Thonburi the new capital.

1782 Rama I moves the royal capital to Bang Makok.

1909 In response to heavy Chinese immigration, Siam requires the adoption of Thai surnames for all citizens.

1910–25 Under King Rama VI, primary education is compulsory.

1932 A bloodless revolution turns Siam into a constitutional monarchy.

1938 Field Marshal Phibul Songkhram becomes the first prime minister; the country's name is changed to Thailand.

1964–73 The US establishes several army bases in Thailand to combat Communist expansion in neighbouring Indochina.

1973 A civilian government, led by academic Kukrit Pramoj, is elected.

1976 After hundreds of protestors are killed at Thammasat University, the Thai military seizes control of the government.

1992 Civilians regain control of the government again.

1997 A steep devaluation of Thai currency leads to an economic crash.

2001 The new Thai Rak Thai (TRT) party sweeps elections.

2006 Military coup unseats Thaksin and the TRT.

2007 TRT party banned, PPP win general elections.

2008 PPP forced out of government.

2009 Pro-Thaksin protests cause the cancellation of ASEAN summit.

2010 Thousands of Red Shirt demonstrators occupy parts of Bangkok, clashing violently with the army.

2011 Thaksin's sister Yingluck becomes Thailand's first female prime minister with the Pheu Thai Party.

2012–13 Pheu Thai's attempt to change the Constitution and create an amnesty is seen as trying to restore Thaksin's assets and allow him to return. Pro- and anti-Thaksin demonstrations continue.

2014 The Constitutional Court removes Yingluck from office. The army launches another coup.

WHERE TO GO

Although the sprawling capital of over 10 million may at first seem daunting, virtually every part of the city is accessible by elevated rail, Metro subway, river and canal boat services or city bus. For any place not easily reached by public transport, taxis are a reasonably priced alternative. Most of the neighbourhoods described here can be explored on foot.

KO RATTANAKOSIN (ROYAL ISLAND)

Resting in a bend of the Chao Phraya River, Bangkok's oldest district contains some of the city's most historic architecture – Wat Phra Kaew, the Grand Palace, Wat Pho and Wat Mahathat, along with the National Museum and the prestigious Thammasat and Silpakorn universities. The river bank in this area is busy with piers and markets, worthwhile attractions in themselves. Despite its name, Ko Rattanakosin is not an island at all, though in the days when Bangkok was known as the 'Venice of the East', Banglamphu Canal and Ong Ang Canal – two lengthy adjoining canals to the east that run parallel to the river – were large enough that the area felt like an island.

Teardrop-shaped Ko Rattanakosin is bounded to the west by the Chao Phraya, to the north by Phra Pin Klao Road and to the east by Atsadang Road and Khlong Lot. The district is accessible by boat via the Tha Chang Chao Phraya river pier, or by road via taxi and public bus.

Grand Palace and Wat Phra Kaew ❶

Also known by the English name, Temple of the Emerald Buddha, and more formally as Wat Phra Si Ratana Satsadaram,

The giant reclining Buddha at Wat Pho

the royal monastery of **Wat Phra Kaew** Ⓐ (daily 8.30am–
3.30pm; entry fee includes admission to Dusit Park) adjoins
the Grand Palace on common ground consecrated in 1782,
the first year of Bangkok rule. The 95-hectare (234-acre) palace
grounds encompass over 100 buildings that represent more
than 200 years of royal history and architectural experimenta-
tion. Most of the architecture is Rattanakosin or Old Bangkok
style. Visitors are forbidden to wear shorts or have bare shoul-
ders, but you can hire clothes for a small fee. Guides and audio
guides can also be hired.

Inside a large chapel heavy with gilded ornamentation,
the 66cm (26in) **Emerald Buddha** Ⓑ (actually carved from
nephrite, a type of jade), after which the *wat* is named, sits in
a miniature glass-paned pavilion with an intricately carved,

The travelling Buddha

Neither the origin nor the sculptor of the Emerald Buddha is known,
but it first appeared in 15th-century Chiang Rai chronicles. Legend says
it was carved in India and brought to Siam via Ceylon, but stylistically it
belongs to northern Thailand's 13th to 14th century Chiang Saen or
Lanna periods. In the 15th century, the Buddha is thought to have been
sealed with plaster and gold leaf and placed in Chiang Rai's own Wat
Phra Kaew. While being carried to a new home, after a storm had damaged the *stupa* (reliquary) containing it, the Buddha lost its covering in
a fall. It then stayed in Lampang for 32 years until it was brought to Wat
Chedi Luang in Chiang Mai.

Lao invaders took the Emerald Buddha from Chiang Mai in the mid-
16th century. General Chakri, later crowned as Rama I, brought it 200
years later to the then Thai capital Thonburi. When Bangkok became the
capital, he moved the Buddha there. The statue has three royal robes,
one each for the hot, rainy and cool seasons, which are changed accord-
ingly by either the king or the crown prince.

five-tiered roof, on a pedestal high above the heads of worshippers. The enigmatic aura of the jade figure is enhanced by the fact that it cannot be examined closely, nor can it be photographed. Its lofty perch emphasises the image's occult significance as the most important talisman of the Thai kingdom and legitimisor of Thai sovereignty.

The other temple structures are equally colourful and include gleaming, gilded *stupas* (Buddhist reliquaries),

Wat Phra Kaew's ornate roof

polished orange-and-green tiled roofs, mosaic-encrusted pillars and rich marble pediments. Extensive murals depicting scenes from the *Ramakien* (the Thai version of the Indian *Ramayana* epic) line the cloisters along the inside walls of the compound. Originally painted during Rama I's reign (1782–1809), the murals have undergone several restorations, including a major one finished in time for the 1982 Bangkok/Chakri dynasty bicentennial. Divided into 178 sections, the murals illustrate the epic in its entirety.

The king's current residence is Chitrlada Palace in the northern part of the city, but the **Grand Palace** **C** (Phra Borom Maharatchawong) is still used by the monarchy for selected ceremonial occasions such as Coronation Day. Although the actual palace is closed to the public, the exteriors of the four buildings are worth a swift perusal.

The largest Grand Palace structure, the triple-winged **Chakri Mahaprasat** **D** (literally 'Great Holy Hall of Chakri', but usually translated as 'Grand Palace Hall') was designed

Chakri Maha Prasat Hall in the Grand Palace complex

by British architects in 1882 and displays a unique blend of traditional Thai and Italian Renaissance architecture, resulting in a style Thais call 'European wearing a Thai classical dancer's headdress', as each of the three wings is roofed with a tiered and heavily ornamented spire. The centrally positioned and tallest of the spires contains the ashes of Chakri kings, while the flanking spires hold those of Chakri princes. Thai kings traditionally housed their huge harems in the Chakri Mahaprasat's innermost halls, under the guard of combat-trained female sentries.

French-inspired **Borombiman Hall** ❺ served as residence for Rama VI, and is still occasionally used to house visiting foreign dignitaries. Originally a hall of justice, **Amarindra Hall** to the west is used only for coronation ceremonies in the present day. Further west stands **Dusit Hall** ❻, originally built for royal audiences but later used as a royal funerary hall.

Wat Pho (Wat Phra Chetuphon)

Wat Pho ❷ (formally known as Wat Phra Chetuphon; daily 8am–5pm; www.watpho.com) is the oldest and largest Buddhist temple in Bangkok and has the longest reclining Buddha in Thailand. The temple site, just south of the palace complex, dates from the 16th century, but the monastery was completely rebuilt in 1781 in preparation for the founding of the new Thai capital the following year.

Chetuphon Road divides the complex into two sections, each enclosed by high whitewashed walls. Only the northern section is open to the public and contains the *wat*'s most famous feature, a huge, gilded reclining Buddha image representing the passing of the Buddha into *parinibbana* (nirvana after death). Measuring 46m (151ft) long and 15m (49ft) high, the figure is made of brick moulded with plaster and finished in shining gold leaf. Mother-of-pearl inlays on the feet display the 108 different auspicious characteristics of a Buddha.

Two smaller sanctuaries to the east of the reclining Buddha contain the beautiful Phra Jinnarat and Phra Jinachi images, both originally cast in Sukhothai in northern Thailand. Galleries linking these chapels with two other chapels are lined with visually striking rows of seated gilded Buddha images, numbering 394 in all.

Rama I's remains are interred in the base of the presiding Buddha image in the main *bot* (ordination hall). Affixed to the lower

The Buddha's giant feet at Wat Pho

At Wat Pho

exterior wall of the *bot* are 152 bas-reliefs, carved in marble and obtained from the ruins of Ayutthaya, depicting scenes from the *Ramakien*. Temple rubbings offered for sale at Wat Pho come from cement casts of these panels.

Other notable structures in the northern compound include four large *stupas* commemorating the first three Chakri kings (Rama III has two *stupas*), 91 smaller *stupas*, an old Tipitaka (Buddhist scripture) library, a sermon hall, a school of Abhidhamma (Buddhist philosophy) and a traditional massage centre.

Wat Pho serves as the national headquarters for the teaching and preservation of traditional Thai medicine, including Thai massage, which is offered to temple visitors for a fee (tel: 0 2622 3533).

Museum of Siam

The **Museum of Siam** (4 Thanon Sanam Chai; tel: 0-2622 2599; Tue–Sun 10am–6pm) is located 150m/yds from Wat Pho's eastern gate. It has inter-active multimedia displays and tableaux explaining what it means to be 'Thai', covering 2,000 years of history, including periods of Khmer, Sukhothai and Ayutthayan dominance. They also have regular temporary exhibitions about Thai culture.

Lak Meuang and Sanam Luang

Bangkok's spiritual centre – and the point of Km 0 for all mapping – is the **Lak Meuang** (City Pillar; free; daily 6am– 6pm), standing across the street from the eastern wall of Wat Phra Kaew. The two-room, crowned pavilion shelters a 3m (9ft), gilded wooden pillar erected in 1782 during the founding of the new capital to worship the city's guardian deity, **Phra Sayam Thewathirat**. During the reign of Rama V, five smaller pillar idols were added to the shrine. The atmosphere of spirit worship is intoxicating, as Bangkokians stream in bearing pig heads and bottles of whisky to offer the spirit, while the shrine musicians hammer away on their wooden xylophones and brass gongs.

Sanam Luang (Royal Field), just north of Wat Phra Kaew, is the traditional site for royal cremations and for the annual Ploughing Ceremony, in which the king or the crown prince officially initiates the rice-growing season.

Before 1982, when it was moved to Chatuchak Park in northern Bangkok, the city's famous Weekend Market convened weekly at Sanam Luang. Nowadays, the large field is used as a picnic and recreational area. A large kite-flying competition is held here during the kite-flying season (Mar–Apr). A **Mae Thorani**

Buddhist insight meditation

The monks at Wat Mahathat practise *satipatthana vipassana* (insight meditation) in the Dhamma Vicaya Hall on most days between 4am and 2pm (call ahead – tel: 0-2222 6011 – to make sure that an English-speaking instructor will be present). Meditation of this kind involves the noting of mental and physical sensations as they arise spontaneously until *vipassana* or insight into the essential nature of reality is acquired. Intensive, long-term residential instruction is also available at the monastery's International Buddhist Meditation Centre (tel: 0-2623 5881; www.mcu.ac.th/IBMC).

Buddhist amulets for sale near Wat Mahathat

statue, representing Dharani (the Hindu-Buddhist earth goddess), occupies a white pavilion at the north end of the field. The 19th-century sculpture marks the site of a former public drinking well.

Wat Mahathat

Opposite Wat Phra Kaew, on the west side of Sanam Luang (Royal Field), **Wat Mahathat** ❸ (daily 7am–6pm) stands close to the Tha Maharat river pier. This large monastery was founded in the 18th century to serve as the national centre for the Mahanikai, the largest of Thailand's two monastic sects. It is also headquarters for Mahathat Rajavidyalaya, one of Thailand's two Buddhist universities and the largest in Southeast Asia, with students from Laos, Vietnam and Cambodia.

While Wat Phra Kaew represents the capital's most elite temple, Wat Mahathat belongs very much to the masses. A daily open-air market features traditional Thai herbal medicine, and out on the street you'll find a string of shops selling herbal cures and offering Thai massage. At weekends, a large produce market held on the temple grounds brings hordes of people. Opposite the main entrance, on the other side of Maharat Road, lies a large Buddhist amulet market.

Nearby **Silpakorn University** is partially housed in a former Rama I palace; Thailand's premier university for arts studies was originally founded as the School of Fine Arts by Italian artist Corrado Feroci (more commonly known by his royally bestowed Thai name, Silpa Bhirasri), who is considered Thailand's father of modern art. A small bookshop just inside the main gate stocks English-language books on Thai art.

National Museum

At the northern end of Na Phra That Road stands the **National Museum** (Wed–Sun 9am–4pm), the largest museum in Southeast Asia and an excellent place to learn about Thai history, art and culture. All historical periods are represented, from Dvaravati (6th–10th century) to Rattanakosin (18th–early 20th century).

The stately buildings, originally built in 1782 as the palace of Rama I's viceroy, were turned into a museum in 1884. In addition to the exhibition halls, the museum grounds contain the restored **Buddhaisawan (Phutthaisawan) Chapel**. The 1795 chapel contains well-preserved original murals and

National Museum

Morning monks

Walk the streets of Bangkok early in the morning, and you'll catch the flash of shaved heads bobbing above bright ochre robes, as monks all over the city engage in *bindabaht*, the daily house-to-house gathering of alms food.

one of the country's most revered Buddha images, the Phra Phuttha Sihing (which is said to come from Ceylon, although the stylistics indicate a 13th-century Sukhothai provenance). One of the more impressive rooms contains a well-maintained collection of traditional musical instruments from Thailand, Laos, Cambodia and Indonesia. Other permanent exhibits include ceramics, clothing and textiles, woodcarving, royal regalia, Chinese art and weaponry.

National Museum volunteers (www.museumvolunteers bkk.net) offer excellent free tours of the museum in English, French, German, Italian and Japanese on Wednesday and Thursday, starting from the ticket pavilion at 9.30am.

Just to the south of the museum, **Thammasat University**, founded in 1934, is the country's most prestigious centre of higher learning for law and political science. The faculty and student body have also long been known for their political activism, and the campus was the site of bloody demonstrations against the Thai military dictatorship of Field Marshal Thanom Kittichorn in October 1976, during which hundreds of Thai students were killed or wounded by right-wing paramilitary groups. A plaque commemorating the incident stands on the field where the violence took place.

CHINATOWN AND AROUND

Bangkok's oldest residential and business district fans along the Chao Phraya River between Tri Phet Road and

Hualamphong Railway Station. Largely inhabited by the descendants of Chinese residents who moved out of Ko Rattanakosin to make way for royal temples and palaces in the early 19th century, the neighbourhood is referred to by Thais as Sampeng (after the longest market lane, Soi Sampeng), or as Yaowarat (after the major avenue bisecting the district). The area includes the Indian market district, Pahurat. Both are best explored on foot, as roads are congested.

Chinatown, off Yaowarat and Ratchawong roads not far from the river, comprises a confusing and crowded array of jewellery, hardware, wholesale food, automotive and fabric shops, as well as dozens of other small businesses. Always effervescent, Chinatown fairly boils over with activity during the annual Vegetarian Festival, when Chinese Thais celebrate the first nine days of the ninth lunar month (September or October) with a culinary orgy of Thai and Chinese vegetarian

Monks receiving alms

Talat Kao market

fare. Bright yellow pennants flutter in front of stalls and cafes to signify that they serve vegetarian food.

The largest and liveliest temple in Chinatown, **Wat Mangkon Kamalawat ❺** (Dragon Lotus Temple), faces onto Charoen Krung Road among shop-houses selling fruit, cakes, incense and ritual burning paper for offerings at the temple. Chinese and Tibetan inscriptions at the entrance give a brief history, while the labyrinthine interior features a succession of Mahayana Buddhist, Taoist and Confucian altars. Virtually day and night, this temple is packed with worshippers lighting incense, filling the ever-burning altar lamps with oil and praying to their ancestors.

Just to the east, **Soi Itsaranuphap ❻** crosses Charoen Krung Road, piercing into Chinatown's main market area. It is flanked with vendors selling ready-to-eat and preserved foodstuffs, including cleaned fish and poultry. Though not for the squeamish, it's one of the cleanest fresh markets in Bangkok.

Down the lane, now across Yaowarat Road, looms the Chinese-lantern-hung entrance to **Talat Kao** (Talat Leng Buay La), a market that's been in continuous operation for over two centuries. All manner and size of freshwater and saltwater fish and shellfish are displayed here, alive and filleted. Continuing towards the river, Itsaranuphap Alley crosses famous **Sampeng Lane** ❼ (Soi Wanit 1), the most crowded of Chinatown's market lanes, a gridlock of pedestrians, pushcarts and the occasional motorbike twisting through the crowds. Shops along this section of Sampeng Lane sell dry goods, especially shoes, clothing, fabric, toys and kitchenware.

Gold shops line **Yaowarat Road**, and for price and selection, this is probably the best place in Thailand to purchase a gold chain (sold by the *baht*, a 15g unit of weight).

In the 1920s and 1930s, Thai and foreign architects blended European Art Deco with functionalist restraint to create Thai Art Deco. Fully realised examples of this form can be found along Chinatown's main streets, particularly Yaowarat Road. Vertical towers over the main doorways are often surmounted with whimsical Deco-style sculptures – the Eiffel Tower, a lion, an elephant, a Moorish dome.

Perched on the top of a commercial building in **Songwat Road**, near Tha Ratchawong, is a rusting model of a World War II vintage Japanese Zero warplane, undoubtedly placed there by the Japanese during their brief 1941 occupation of Bangkok; in style and proportion it fits the surrounding Thai Art Deco elements.

Weighing tea at a Chinatown tea shop

Pahurat

At the western edge of Chinatown, Sampeng Lane leads to **Chakraphet Road**, the beginning of Pahurat, a district dominated by Indian-owned fabric shops. Chakraphet Road itself is well known for its Indian restaurants and shops selling

Thai Art Deco

Surviving examples of Thai Art Deco include the Chalermkrung Royal Theatre, the Royal Hotel, Ratchadamnoen Boxing Stadium and the General Post Office.

Indian sweets. In a back alley on the west side of the road stands **Sri Gurusingh Sabha**, a large Sikh temple. Open to visitors, it claims to be the second-largest Sikh temple outside of India. Behind the temple, and stretching westward to Triphet Road, **Pahurat Market ❽** is devoted almost exclusively to textiles and clothing. At the southern end of Tri Phet Road, the colourful **Pak Khlong Talad ❾** (Flower Market) is particularly lively at night, a time when young Thais flock to the adjoining Saphan Phut Market for a wide selection of wares, including clothes and accessories.

Eastern Chinatown and Hualamphong

At the eastern edge of Chinatown near the intersection of Yaowarat and Charoen Krung roads, close to Hualamphong Railway Station, is **Wat Traimit ❿** (Temple of the Golden Buddha; daily 8am–5pm). A huge, 600 million-baht, marble mondop (pavilion) here contains an impressive 3m (10ft) high seated Buddha image cast in solid gold. Moulded in the graceful Sukhothai style and weighing 5.5 tonnes, the image was 'rediscovered' some 40 years ago beneath a plaster exterior when it toppled from a crane while being transported to a new building in the compound. The covering may have been added to protect it from invading armies either during the Sukhothai or Ayutthaya periods. Although the temple site here may date from the early 13th century, Wat Traimit certainly took its current form no more than 200 years ago. Also inside the mondop is the Yaowarat Chinatown Heritage Centre (daily 8am–4.30pm), which relates the story of Chinatown through old photos, prints of period paintings and tableaux of such things as the interior of a junk and shops from old Sampeng Lane. The well annotated exhibits give interesting context to an area visit.

Bangkok's **Hualamphong Railway Station**, built by Dutch architects and engineers just before World War I, represents one of the city's earliest and most outstanding examples of Thai Art Deco. The vaulted iron roof and neoclassical portico demonstrate state-of-the-art engineering for the time, while the patterned, two-toned skylights exemplify De Stijl Dutch modernism.

Towards the southeastern edge of Chinatown, a 19th-century Chinese entrepreneur built what is now **Talat Noi** (Little Market), where larger riverboats could offload wholesale goods. Going south down Soi Charoen Phan, turn right into Soi Duang Tawan to reach **Chao Sua Son's home.** Look for the car park 50 metres/yards on the left and go through the doorway marked Green Diver. It's a functioning dive school, but no one minds if you look around the evocative old Chinese building and surrounding courtyard. It is one of very few surviving examples of traditional Chinese residential architecture in Thailand.

Talat Noi serves as a cultural and geographic bridge between the almost

In Wat Traimit

At Hualamphong
Railway Station

exclusively Chinese ambience of Yaowarat Chinatown to the north and what in the 19th century was the almost exclusively Western district of European trading houses and embassies to the immediate south.

As the palace treasury struggled with the complexities of burgeoning international trade, King Rama IV granted a licence to establish the Book (as in 'bookkeeping') Club further south on Soi Charoen Phan. The name was later changed to **Siam Commercial Bank**, today one of Thailand's three top banks. The early 20th-century, Italian Rennaisance style bank still functions, its tellers seated behind old-fashioned iron-grill windows, with the bank vault lying beneath the original tiled floor.

Close by stands the **Holy Rosary Church** ⓫, built in 1787 by Portuguese residents and the capital's oldest place of Christian worship. The original wood structure was replaced with the neo-Gothic stucco building after an 1890 fire. Known in Thai as Wat Kalawan, from the Portuguese 'Calvario' (Calvary), the church features a Romanesque single-tower façade, stained-glass windows, gilded ceilings and a very old, life-sized Jesus effigy, which is carried in the streets during Easter processions.

One hundred metres south lies River City Shopping Complex.

THONBURI

In the mid-16th century, during the height of Ayutthaya's power, forward-looking Thai merchants transformed the wooded western bank of the Chao Phraya River into an important trade entrepôt called Thonburi Si Mahasamut. When Ayutthaya fell to the Burmese in 1767, Siamese troops and the royal court shifted to Thonburi, which served as the capital of the Siamese kingdom for a brief 15 years.

Although today Thonburi comprises nearly half of metropolitan Bangkok in size and population, it is barely beginning the development of the more modern cityscape on the opposite bank.

Thonburi canals

A vast network of **canals** criss-cross Thonburi in multiple directions, moving cargo and passengers, and providing a seemingly endless source of water for bathing, cooking, irrigation and recreation. Crowded water taxis weave among 'longtail' boats (named after the 3m/10ft propeller shafts jutting from the stern), ancient teak ferries and huge iron barges heaped with gravel or rice and chained together.

A longtail trip west off the Chao Phraya into **Bangkok Noi Canal** ⑫ to the north

Building the canals

Using thousands of Khmer prisoners of war, King Rama I augmented Bangkok's natural canal-and-river system with hundreds of artificial waterways. All fed into Thailand's hydraulic lifeline, the broad Chao Phraya River, which bisected the city centre into two halves, Bangkok proper and Thonburi, the river's 'right bank'.

seems to knock 50 years off big city progress, as the scenery transforms from high-rises into a snug corridor of teak houses on stilts, old Buddhist temples and banana groves. Thai women in straw lampshade-shaped hats hawk steaming bowls of rice noodles from wooden canoes. Mobile banks and post offices putter along atop tiny barges, further demonstrating that virtually any errand one might accomplish on land can also be done on water.

Bangkok Noi Canal links up with Bang Yai Canal, site of **Wat Intharam**, where a *stupa* enshrines the ashes of Phaya Taksin. Fine *lai kham* (gold-and-black lacquerwork) adorning the chapel doors depicts a mythical tree which bears fruit in the shape of beautiful maidens.

From Bangkok Noi Canal, you can continue by boat up **Om Canal**, lined by plantations growing the spiky, strong-smelling durian. Another turn in the maze links up with **Mon Canal**, and you whoosh past gold-spired temples, century-old wooden piers and hothouses filled with exotic orchids.

Royal Barges National Museum

The Thai custom of royal boat processions dates to at least the reign of King Prasat Thong (1630–55) in the late Ayutthaya period, and Thailand's current royal dynasty has maintained the latest fleet of majestic river vessels for nearly a century. The long, fantastically ornamented boats are still employed for ceremonial processions on the river. When not in use the watercraft are kept on public display in sheds that are part of the **Royal Barges National Museum** ⑬ (9am–5pm) on Bangkok Noi Canal, near its junction with the Chao Phraya River, not far from Phra Pin Klao Bridge.

Suphannahong, the King's personal barge, measures 50m (164ft) in length and is carved from a single piece of timber, making it the largest dugout in the world. The name means 'golden swan', and navigation requires a rowing crew of 50 men, plus seven umbrella-bearers, two helmsmen, two naviga-tors, as well as a flagman, rhythm-keeper and chanter. A huge swan head has been carved into the bow and gilded. Lesser royal barges on display feature bows carved into *naga* (sea dragon) and *garuda* (Vishnu's bird mount) shapes.

Every year during the royal *kathin* (when new robes are offered to Buddhist monks) at the end of the annual Rains Retreat, the barges take to the river in a grand procession.

Forensic Medicine Museum

On the ground floor of the Forensic Medicine Building at Siriraj Hospital (on Phrannok Road, near Bangkok Noi Railway Station), the **Forensic Medicine Museum** ⑭ (Wed–Mon 10am–5pm) is the most famous of the 10 medical museums on the hospital premises. Grisly displays include the preserved bodies of some of the most famous

Life on the water

Thai murderers (including Si Ouey, Thailand's equivalent of Jack the Ripper), clever murder weapons and other crime-related memorabilia.

Wat Arun

The striking **Wat Arun** ⑮, or Temple of Dawn (www.wat arun.net; daily 8.30am–5.30pm), named after Aruna, the Indian god of dawn, features the tallest *stupa* in Bangkok and is probably the most photographed monument in the city after Wat Phra Kaew. An older monastery, 17th-century Wat Jang, once shared this site with Phaya Taksin's royal palace when Thonburi was the Thai capital, harbouring the Emerald Buddha before Rama I moved it across the river to Bangkok.

Bangkok's waterworld

Portuguese priest Fernão Mendez Pinto was the first to use the epithet 'Venice of the East', referring not to Bangkok but to Ayutthaya, in a letter to the Society of Jesus in Lisbon in 1554. Three hundred years later it came to be used to describe the new Bangkok capital as well, as in 1855, British envoy Sir John Bowring noted: 'The highways of Bangkok are not streets or roads but the river and the canals. Boats are the universal means of conveyance and communication.'

On the eve of the coronation of Rama VI in 1911, a young and adventurous Italian nobleman named Salvatore Besso wrote:

'The Venice of the Far East – the capital still wrapped in mystery, in spite of the thousand efforts of modernism amid its maze of canals… [T]he crowded dock-roads of the River… which reminds one of the Giudecca… the canals ploughed by sampans, which the rowers guide standing as in Venice… little bridges and tiny gardens, reflecting in the quiet water the drooping foliage of ancient trees… as in the remotest corners of the City of the Doges…'

Wat Arun by night

The 82m (270ft) *stupa*, constructed during the first half of the 19th century during the reigns of Rama II and Rama III, represents a unique design that elongates the typical Khmer 'corn cob' *stupa* tower into a distinctly more slender, Thai shape. The plaster covering the *stupa*'s brick core is embedded with a mosaic of broken, multi-hued Chinese porcelain, a common temple ornamentation in the early Rattanakosin period, when Chinese ships calling at Bangkok used tonnes of old porcelain as ballast. Steep stairs reach a lookout point about halfway up with fine views of Thonburi and the river.

Inside the ordination hall sits a large Buddha image said to have been designed by Rama II, whose ashes are contained in the base of the image. The walls are richly painted with Buddhist murals dating from Rama V's reign.

The grassy monastery grounds near the river make a peaceful retreat, and at night hundreds of lights illuminate the outline of the *stupa*, making it visible from a wide radius.

Santa Cruz Church

Santa Cruz Church

Portuguese Catholic missionaries were among the first Europeans to reside in Siam, first in Ayutthaya and later Bangkok. In 1770, they accepted a land grant in Thonburi from Phaya Taksin and built a simple wooden church known in Thai as **Kuti Jeen** (Chinese Cloister, since most of the congregation were Chinese converts). As the Portuguese presence diminished, the church gradually fell into disrepair until it was renovated in 1835 and renamed **Santa Cruz Church** ⑯ (open Sat–Sun only; free). In 1913 the wooden church was demolished and replaced with a larger and more solid brick edifice that remains in use today, trimmed in maroon and cream, with a domed belfry and stained-glass windows. A spacious courtyard contains a tidy garden, a statue of the Virgin Mary and a large crucifix. The associated **Santa Cruz Convent School** is considered one of the capital's better non-government schools.

OLD BANGKOK

While Ko Rattanakosin was almost exclusively reserved for Thai nobility, areas to the east and north of Ko Rattanakosin were origin-ally occupied by important government departments, commercial enterprises with royal connections and high-ranking monasteries. **Old Bangkok** (Banglamphu) still retains much of that character in parts, while a newer bohemian culture has filled other areas – Khao San Road, for example.

Wat Suthat

Begun by Rama I and completed by Rama II and Rama III, **Wat Suthat**  (daily 8.30am–9pm) has a chapel containing several impressive gilded Buddha images, including Phra Si Sakayamuni, Thailand's largest Sukhothai-period bronze, along with jewel-toned murals chronicling tales from the Buddha's life. The main sanctuary is fitted with large wooden doors carved by various artisans of the period, including King Rama II himself. The ashes of Rama VIII (Ananda Mahidol, the current king's deceased older brother) are enshrined in the base of the presiding Buddha image.

Close to Wat Suthat stand two Brahmanist shrines, the **Thewa Sathan** (Deva Sthan) across the street to the northwest and the smaller **San Chao Phitsanu** (Vishnu Shrine) to the east. The former contains images of Shiva and Ganesha, while the latter is dedicated to Vishnu. These shrines hold a special place in the Thai spirituality because of their resident Brahman priests. The white-robed, Thai-Indian celibates perform important annual ceremonies, such as the Royal Ploughing Ceremony in May, on behalf of the entire nation.

Buddhas at Wat Suthat

The Giant Swing

Close to Wat Suthat, **Sao Ching-Cha** (Giant Swing) was once the site of an astonishing Brahman festival in honour of the Hindu God Shiva each year. Participants would swing high above the ground in ever-higher arcs while trying to grab a bag of gold suspended from a 15m (50ft) bamboo pole. Many died trying, and during the reign of Rama VII (1925–35) the custom was halted.

Monk's Bowl Village (Ban Baht)

During the reign of the first Chakri monarch, Rama I (1782–1809), Siam's new royal capital dedicated three villages in Bangkok to the making of alms bowls for use by Buddhist monks to gather food from laypeople during their morning alms rounds. Today only one, **Ban Baht** ⑱ (Monk's Bowl Village), survives, along a single narrow alley.

The average bowl-smith can only make one bowl a day, hammering out eight strips of metal in the traditional manner, fusing them in a wood fire with pellets of copper, then polishing the bowl and coating it with multiple layers of black lacquer. Only about half a dozen families still make the traditional alms bowls, and most of them are sold to wealthy Thais or tourists, as they are much more expensive than modern factory-made ones.

To find the village, walk south on Boriphat Road, south of Bamrung Meuang Road, then left on Soi Ban Baht. As you go along, you can browse the long rows of shops selling monks' robes and alms bowls.

The Golden Mount

Wat Saket is an undistinguished Rattanakosin-style temple famous only because of the **Golden Mount** ❿ (Phu Khao Thong; daily 7.30am–5.30pm) in the western portion of the compound. A century ago it would have been the highest point in Bangkok, offering unparallelled views of the city below, and still today, because of the lack of any high-rise buildings in the immediate vicinity, it's worth a climb for views of the local rooftops.

This hill was never natural and in fact was originally intended to be a large *stupa*. Construction began under Rama III (1824–51), but when the base collapsed because the soft soil couldn't support it, the brick *stupa* was abandoned. Rama IV (1851–68) later constructed a much smaller one atop the weed-choked mound of ruins. When the British government gave Thailand a Buddha relic from India, Rama V (1868–1910) renovated the *stupa* to house the holy object, bringing the Golden Mount to its current height of 76m

Old fortifications

Open trade with the Portuguese, Dutch, English, French and Chinese had made Bangkok's fortifications obsolete by the mid-19th century, and most of the city's original wall was demolished to make way for sealed roadways.

Democracy Monument

(250ft). To prevent erosion, concrete walls were added in the 1940s.

Wat Saket hosts one of Bangkok's largest temple festivals each November or December (depending on lunar phase) to honour the Buddha relic in the Golden Mount *stupa*. A candlelit procession up the hills marks the festival's high point.

The 7km (4-mile) long Banglamphu Canal curves gently inland from the river towards another wall-and-bunker cluster, **Mahakan Fort** (8.30am–6pm; free), marking the eastern edge of Old Bangkok. Of the 4m (13ft) high, 3m (10ft) thick ramparts that once lined the entire canal, only Phra Sumen (see page 55) and Mahakan have been preserved to remind us what 18th-century Bangkok really was about – keeping foreign armies at bay. Nearby is a small green park overlooking Ong Ang Canal.

Another 50m/yds west on Ratchadamnoen Road is the Rattanakosin Exhibition Hall (100 Thanon Ratchadamnoen Klang; tel: 0-2621 0044; www.nitasrattanakosin. com; Tue–Fri 11am–8pm, Sat–Sun 10am–8pm), which portrays the official history of the area. It has multimedia displays including architecture, traditional arts and the Grand Palace, and visitors can learn some *khon* masked dance and puppetry skills.

Democracy Monument

In 1939 the prime minister Phibul Songkhram chose Ratchadamnoen Road – originally designed for royal motorcades – as the site for **Democracy Monument ⑳** commemorating the 1932 revolution that replaced Thailand's absolute monarchy with a constitutional one. The designer Feroci and his students from Bangkok's School of Fine Arts erected four Art Deco flanges to symbolise the cooperation of the army, air force, navy and police in the coup. Their 24m (79ft) height signifies the day of the coup, 24 June, while 75 cannonballs in the base encode the year, BE 2475 (AD 1932). Bas-relief scenes depict the original coup leaders, the Thai people, the armed forces and a bucolic scene portraying 'Balance and Good Life'. In the centre a bullet-shaped turret enshrines a bronze casting of the 1932 constitution.

October 14 Memorial and Museum

This amphitheatre and museum commemorate the tragic events of 14 October 1973, when the Thai military fired upon a 500,000-strong crowd of pro-democracy protestors at the Democracy Monument, killing over 70. The demonstrators were protesting against the arrest of 13 students who had demanded a democratic constitution from Field Marshal Thanom Kittikachorn. Public revulsion at the massacre led to free elections in January 1975. The centrepiece of the memorial is a contemporary, secular interpretation of a Buddhist *stupa* made from granite blocks, built on the site of the former Thai TV

Mahakan Fort

Arriving on the hectic Khao San Road

News Agency, which had burned to the ground during the demonstrations. The walls of the adjacent elevated amphitheatre are decorated with historic pro-democracy posters and photographs taken on that fateful day. A spiral staircase leads underground to a library and **museum** displaying such historical memorabilia as the 16mm camera which student Shin Khlai-Pan used to record some of the 14 October 1973 events and the famous beret worn by protest organiser Seksan Prasertkul as he led the crowd down Ratchadamnoen Avenue.

Khao San Road
Well-to-do farmers and merchants from Ayutthaya who followed the royal court to Bangkok in the late 18th century settled in Banglamphu – in the northern part of Old Bangkok – a reference to the lamphu tree (Duabanga grandiflora) once common to the area. By the time of Rama IV (1851–68), Banglamphu had become a flourishing commercial district,

and **Khao San Road** ㉑ was lined with two-storey shop-houses with a few teak mansions mixed in. By the early 1980s, two Chinese-Thai hotels on the road had been discovered by the European, American and Australian backpackers, and within a decade there were close to 100 guesthouses in the immediate vicinity (and today there are hundreds more).

Most of the two-storey shop-houses have been replaced by budget hotels, music and souvenir shops, restaurants, internet cafés, tattoo parlours and myriad other services orientated towards the young and peripatetic. At night the street is closed off to vehicular traffic and a circus-cum-market atmosphere prevails, with vendors selling everything from colourful neo-hippie garb to *phat thai* (Thai-style fried noodles).

Phra Sumen Fort and Santichaiprakan Park

Standing on the banks of the Chao Phraya River in Banglamphu, off Phra Athit Road, **Phra Sumen Fort** ㉒ (daily 5am–10pm) is named after Buddhist mythology's Mount Sumeru. The octagonal brick-and-stucco city fort was erected in 1783 as a defence against naval invasion and is one of only two remaining of the original 14 forts dotted along the Banglamphu Canal.

The adjoining **Santichaiprakan Park** is a favourite riverside spot for locals to picnic. A stroll along the cement walkway south from the park takes you past a handful of impressive residences built by Bangkok aristocrats in the late 19th and early 20th centuries. Today, most have been converted into headquarters for the Buddhist Society of Thailand, UNESCO and other non-profit organisations.

DUSIT

Dusit, an area centred around the royal palaces, associated outbuildings and extensive gardens, was inspired by Rama

Abhisek Dusit Throne Hall's
striking porticoes

V's 1897 tour of Europe, particularly France and England. Upon his return the king and his courtiers decided that the former Grand Palace by the river was too cramped and old-fashioned, so they set about transforming an area of fruit orchards, extending Padung Krung Kasem and Samsen canals into an ambitious royal esplanade. Construction on Suan Dusit (Dusit Park) and the new palace began in 1900, and when completed in 1915 the complex encompassed three throne halls and 13 royal residences set among landscaped grounds covering 76 hectares (188 acres).

After the 1932 revolution ended absolute monarchy, and as 20th-century Bangkok began modernising, the crown relinquished much of the original palace grounds to commercial development in the area. The present Suan Dusit is thus about half the size it was when originally established, and many royal promenades are today lined with government offices, schools and residential blocks. Still the area carries an air of grandeur and respect for the monarchy, with less of the urban chaos common in other precincts.

Dusit Park

The main southern entrance into **Dusit Park** ㉓ (daily 9.30am–4pm; free for Grand Palace ticket-holders), now open to the public as the current king resides at the newer Chitrlada Palace nearby, is marked by Royal Plaza, a large roundabout at the end of Ratchadamnoen Road.

In the centre of the roundabout stands a bronze equestrian **statue of Rama V**. Although originally placed here as a mere historical monument, over the last two decades the statue has become the object of a devotional cult with the belief that the king's spirit resides at this spot.

Behind Royal Plaza, the **Ananda Samakhom Throne Hall** is an Italian revival masterpiece designed by Italian architects Annibale Rigotti and Mario Tamagno. The domed hall housed the Thai parliament after the 1932 revolution.

Beyond the throne hall lies the pièce de résistance of Dusit Park, **Vimanmek Mansion** (www.vimanmek.com; Tue–Sun,

Rama V cult

The veneration of Rama V (aka King Chulalongkorn, 1868–1910) dates back to the 1991 military coup and the 1990–2 economic recession, when many Thais became disillusioned with politics and began looking for a new spiritual outlet with historical relevancy. The middle classes seized on Rama V, who, without the help of a parliament or the military, had brought Thai nationalism to the fore while fending off European colonisation. He is also revered for his abolition of slavery.

In Bangkok, the most visible devotional activities are focused on the bronze statue of Rama V in Royal Plaza, which has been transformed into a religious shrine. Every Tuesday, from 9pm until early in the morning, thousands of Bangkokians come to offer candles, flowers, incense and bottles of whisky to the newly ordained demigod.

Ironically, few Rama V devotees realise that the king conceded substantial Thai territory to French Indochina and British Malaya during his reign. Rama V also deserves more credit for the nation's Westernisation than any other monarch, being the first king to travel to Europe (in 1897 and 1907). After seeing Europeans eating with forks, knives and spoons, he discouraged the Thai tradition of taking food with the hands. He also introduced the use of chairs.

9am–3.15pm; one-hour guided tours only, every half-hour in several languages). Rama V originally built this beautiful Victorian mansion on the island of Ko Si Chang in 1868. Later, because the Gulf of Thailand was deemed vulnerable to French invasion, Vimanmek was moved to its present site in 1910. The extraordinary L-shaped, three-storey residence contains 81 rooms, halls and anterooms, along with dozens of grand staircases, and is said to be the world's largest golden teak building. Rooms display Rama V's personal effects as well as an impressive collection of early Rattanakosin art and antiques. The tours cover around 30 rooms. Traditional Thai classical and folk dances are performed at 10.30am and 2pm in a pavilion off the canal side of the mansion.

Nearby, **Abhisek Dusit Throne Hall** is a smaller wood and brick-and-stucco building, opened in 1904 to receive visiting dignitaries. Typical of the finer architecture of the era, the Victorian-influenced gingerbread and Moorish porticoes blend to create a striking and distinctly Thai exterior. The hall displays traditional Thai arts and crafts, sponsored by the Promotion of Supplementary Occupations and Related Techniques (SUPPORT), a royal foundation under the patronage of Queen Sirikit.

Vimanmek Mansion is the world's largest golden teak building

Two elephant stables that once housed three 'white' elephants – animals whose relatively pale hide and auspicious markings meant they would be automatically offered to the king – have been converted into the **Royal Elephant Museum**. Exhibits of photos, tools and artefacts associated

Ananda Samakhom Throne Hall

with Thai elephant lore are on display, as well as the ranking system for the royal elephants. In one of the stables stands a life-like sculpture of one of the most important royal elephants (now kept at the Chitrlada Palace).

Two residence halls to the north of Vimanmek are now used to house the **HM King Bhumiphol Photography Exhibitions**, a collection of the king's photography, as well as photos of the king and the royal family.

Nearby, **Princess Orathai Thep Kanya Residential Hall** contains rare and beautiful silk and cotton textiles that were woven during the reigns of Rama IV and Rama V.

Other palace-complex structures open to the public include the **Suan Kularb Residential Hall and Throne Hall**, once home to King Rama V's son Prince Atsdang Dejavudh. The two red-roofed buildings appear to blend Tudor, Victorian and Swiss chalet elements. Today, they're used to display the king's collection of paintings (some painted by His Majesty, some by other artists).

Near the north entrance to Dusit Park, the **Royal Carriage Museum** has 13 royal horse carriages (for the king and queen) and palanquins (for courtiers) that were used by the court of Rama V in the pre-automobile era.

Suan Si Rue Di, a more traditional Thai residence raised on stilts and featuring exterior stairways and hipped roofs trimmed with Victorian details, once served as a residence for Queen Saovabha and Princess Valaya Alongkorn (aunt to the current king). The hall features a collection of gifts that were presented to King Bhumibol on the 50th and 60th anniversaries of his coronation.

Tamnak Ho was built for Rama V's son Prince Paribatra Sukhumbandhu, but today houses 13th-century Sukhothai ceramics salvaged from Gulf of Thailand shipwrecks. This residence was moved from another part of the city to its present position in 1998.

Suan Bua, formerly a home for Princess Saisavali Bhiromya, one of Rama V's favourite consorts, contains a striking collection of Buddha images, historic photographs from the Rama VI era, and gifts presented to King Bhumibol by visiting heads of state.

Krom Luang Vorased Thasuda Residential Hall, once home to Rama III's daughter Princess Bootri, is used for an exhibit of ancient pottery from Ban Chiang, a civilisation that flourished in northeastern Thailand 4,000 to 8,000 years ago.

Dusit Zoo

Rama VIII gave his private botanical garden, Khao Din Wana, to the people of Bangkok in 1938 for the purpose of creating a zoological garden. Located between Chitrlada Palace and the National Assembly Hall, with the main entrance off Ratwithi Road, the 19-hectare (47-acre) **Dusit Zoo** ㉔ (www.dusitzoo. org; 8am–6pm) harbours over 1,600 species of mammals, reptiles and birds, including relatively rare indigenous species and one of the best collections of gibbons anywhere in the world.

Even for visitors not particularly interested in the animal kingdom, the zoo makes a pleasant retreat from city noise and dust. Plants and trees in the ample grounds are labelled in English, Thai and Latin, and an artificial lake in the centre offers paddleboats for rent. A small fun park with a playground and amusement park rides will help entertain small children. Lakeside restaurants serve inexpensive Thai food. Weekdays are much less crowded than weekends.

In Dusit Zoo

CENTRAL BANGKOK

A nexus of upscale hotels, plush shopping malls, state-of-the-art cinemas, foreign embassies, the National Stadium and Thailand's most prestigious university, central Bangkok is a magnet for both Thai residents and visiting foreigners.

Jim Thompson's House

Jim Thompson's House ㉕ (Soi Kasem San 2, Rama I Road; www.jimthompsonhouse.com; daily 9am–5pm), just north of the National Stadium Skytrain station, is the former residence

Jim Thompson's House

of American silk entrepreneur Jim Thompson, who almost single-handedly popularised Thai silk worldwide.

Thompson, an architect by training, joined the Office of Strategic Services, which later became the CIA, and served in Thailand for a brief time. When he was discharged, he took a commission to renovate the now famous Oriental Hotel, before founding his Thai Silk Company in 1947. The company profited, as his renditions of traditional Thai silk colours and patterns – which at the time were in danger of disappearing – became popular in the Milan, London and Paris fashion worlds.

Thompson became an avid collector of Thai and Southeast Asian art, and was one of the first Westerners living in Thailand to become interested in traditional Thai teak homes. Collecting six derelict houses in central Thailand, he reassembled them in 1959 to create one of the most envied residential compounds in Bangkok.

The silk king mysteriously disappeared in 1967, while walking on holiday in Malaysia's Cameron Highlands. Despite massive search efforts, no trace of him was ever found. The Thai government turned Thompson's sumptuous residence, complete with his collection of art and antiques, into a museum, including a gallery, silk showroom and café.

Bangkok Art and Culture Centre

East along Rama I Rd is the Bangkok Art and Culture Centre (939 Rama I Road; tel: 0-2214 6630–8; www.bacc. or.th; free), Bangkok's largest gallery. The 11-storey space has no permanent exhibition, but stages some of the city's best local and international art and multimedia shows. It also hosts live performances, art markets, retail outlets and organisations such as the Thai Film Foundation and Bangkok Opera.

Siam Square

To the southeast, on the other side of Phaya Thai Road, **Siam Square 26**, a grid of 12 short lanes, is where Bangkok's cutting edge blends into trendiness, forged into Thai pop culture by television and the other mass media. At weekends in particular, Siam Square draws hordes of Thai teenagers who hang out in local cafés and noodle shops. The land here is owned by Chulalongkorn University, and with the overspill of students Siam Square was for many years a hotbed of young fashion designers

Inside Jim Thompson's House

taking their first steps into the industry. While there are still elements of this sub-culture, the streetside ambiance has been transformed by the rapid rise of large shopping malls.

South of Siam Square, **Chulalongkorn University**, founded in 1917 by Rama VI, is the kingdom's oldest and most selective university. The older buildings on campus, a blend of Rattanakosin and Italian revival architecture, surround a grassy parade ground and a seated statue of Rama V (King Chulalongkorn), after whom the university was named. The cultural centre for student performing arts is home to the **Jamjuree Art Gallery**, which hosts changing exhibits of student artwork.

Busy Siam Square

Siam Square and MBK, opposite on Phaya Thai Road, mark the beginning of Bangkok's modern downtown shopping district, a series of upmarket malls stretching for several kilometres along Rama I Rd.

Wang Suan Pakkard

North of Rama I Road, on Sri Ayutthaya Road, Prince Chumbhot and his wife Mom Ratchawong Pantip brought five 19th-century Thai houses down from Chiang Mai and reassembled them in 1952 to serve as their residence. The prince added a sixth teak structure from a monastery in Ayutthaya in 1958, and two contemporary buildings were built later to house the royal couple's extensive collection of art and artefacts. Known as **Wang Suan Pakkard** ㉗ (www.suanpakkad. com; daily 9am–4pm), or Cabbage Farm Palace, the eight houses are filled with historic Thai Buddha images, Ban Chiang ceramics, Khmer Hindu-Buddhist art and antique furnishings.

The Ayutthaya-style monastery chapel, popularly known as the **Lacquer Pavilion**, is famous for its sumptuous gold-leaf-on-lacquer murals illustrating episodes from the *Ramakien*, the life stories of the Buddha and scenes from daily Ayutthaya life.

Thap Thim Shrine

Moving east, close to Petchaburi Road, at the back of the Swissôtel Nai Lert Park on Withayu Road, is the unusual **Thap Thim Shrine**. It consists of clusters of carved stone and wooden phalluses surrounding a spirit house built by Bangkok millionaire Nai Lert in homage to Chao Mae Thap Thim, a female spirit believed to inhabit a large banyan tree behind. According to legend, a woman who left an offering of a wooden phallus here asking to get pregnant had her wish granted. Word spread, other women seeking fertility began doing the same and the shrine is now overflowing with phalluses, in all shapes, sizes and colours.

Erawan Shrine

Back to the south, on the corner of Ratchaprarop and Ploenchit roads, next to the Grand Hyatt Erawan Hotel, stands the **Erawan Shrine** ㉘, originally built to ward off bad luck during the construction of the original Erawan Hotel (torn down to make way for the Grand Hyatt some years ago). The four-headed deity at the centre of the shrine is Brahma, the Hindu god of creation. At first a typical Thai spirit house was erected, but was replaced with the Brahma shrine after several mishaps delayed the hotel construction. Worshippers who have a wish granted may return to commission the musicians and dancers who are always ready to perform.

Lumphini Park

South of the Erawan Shrine, Bangkok's oldest public park, **Lumphini Park** 🉐 (daily 5am–8pm) was established on crown land given to the city by Rama VI in 1925. He invited farmers and merchants to mount an exhibition of local products and natural resources for a year, and afterwards named the 14-hectare (35-acre) grounds Lumphini Park (the Thai pronunciation of Lumbini, the birthplace of the Buddha in Nepal).

Called 'Suan Lum' by locals, the park is bounded by Rama IV, Ratchadamri and Withayu roads. Interspersed among spacious grassy tracts stand the city's oldest public library (8am–8pm), a dance hall, a senior citizens' club, a youth centre, a tea shop and a weight lifting area. A statue of Rama VI stands at the southwestern entrance to the park. From mid-February until April, during the kite-flying season, the park is full of kites, which are also available to buy here. Visit Suan Lum in the early morning to see local residents practising t'ai chi, drinking tea and herbal tonics or jogging along the network of pathways.

Worshipping at Erawan Shrine

Since 2010, the park has been the site of several demonstrations in Thailand's political upheavals.

Snake Farm

Formerly known as the Pasteur Institute, and more

Relaxing in Lumphini Park

commonly called the Snake Farm, the Thai Red Cross-sponsored **Queen Saovabha Memorial Institute** (Phra Ram IV Road; Mon–Fri 8.30am–4.30pm, Sat–Sun 8.30am–noon) is just west of Lumphini Park. It is a favourite stop for visitors keen to see the milking of Thailand's six venomous snake species – common cobra, king cobra, banded krait, Malayan pit viper, green pit viper and Russell's viper. The snakes, raised in captivity, are milked daily to produce snake-bite antidotes, which are distributed to clinics and hospitals throughout Thailand. Founded in 1923, the institute became the second antivenin research facility in the world, after one in Brazil. Unlike other 'snake farms' in Bangkok, this is a serious herpetological research facility, named after Rama V's queen, a pioneer in promoting health education in Thailand.

The public **milking sessions** (weekdays 11am and 2.30pm, weekends and holidays 11am only) are a major Bangkok attraction. An informative half-hour slide show on snakes is

Assumption Cathedral

presented before the milking sessions.

SILOM AND BANGRAK

In the 19th and early 20th centuries, when large sailing ships and steamships would navigate up the Chao Phraya River, the more prominent international trade firms and foreign embassies placed their headquarters on the banks of **Bangrak**, south of Ko Rattanakosin and Chinatown. Serving a primarily foreign clientele, the legendary Oriental Hotel began its career here as a humble riverside lodge in 1865; today it is one of the city's most luxurious temporary addresses.

Alongside European residents, migrants from India and Pakistan conducted their businesses in the gem and fabric trades, and still do so today in the many shops lining **Charoen Krung Road** (the first road in the capital to be sealed, in 1861), which follows the river for 10km (6 miles), linking Bangrak with Old Bangkok.

Heading inland from Charoen Krung, **Silom Road** was also built mainly to serve the Europeans and South Asians. Instead of trade and shipping concerns, businesses along here were focused on banking, finance and insurance. Later on, Silom Road (and parallel Surawong Road) became a popular location for airline offices and hotels, which led to the development of the famous red-light district of Patpong.

Close to where Silom and Charoen Krung roads meet stands the Cathedral of the Assumption of the Blessed Mary, or the **Assumption Cathedral** ㉚, as it's generally known. French missionaries became influential in Bangkok in the 19th century and built a Catholic church on this site, close to the river, in 1822. This was replaced by a larger Romanesque church between 1910 and 1918, which was badly damaged in World War II. The church was promoted to cathedral status in 1965, and in 1984 Pope John Paul II said Mass here. The cathedral is found on the same lane as the famous Mandarin **Oriental Hotel** (www.mandarin oriental.com).

Sri Mariamman Temple (Maha Uma Devi Temple)

Called Wat Phra Si Maha Umathewi in Thai (or simply Wat Khaek, 'Indian Temple'), the **Sri Mariamman Temple** ㉛ (daily 6am–8pm; free) sits at the intersection of Silom and Pan roads in Bangrak. Built in the mid-19th century by Tamil immigrants, this Hindu sanctuary features a colourful tower decorated with sculptures of Hindu deities in classical South Indian style. A gold-plated copper dome tops off the tower, and inside the small temple interior is a shrine altar dedicated to Uma Devi (Shiva's consort), flanked by shrines for her elephant-headed son Ganesha and her son Khanthakumara. For good measure, lesser

The intricately decorated Sri Mariamman Temple

walls are festooned with figures of Shiva, Vishnu and Buddha. Bright yellow marigold garlands are sold at the entrance for use as offerings.

An interesting ritual takes place in the temple at noon on most days, when a priest brings out a tray carrying an oil lamp, coloured powders and holy water. He sprinkles the water on the hands of worshippers, who in turn pass their hands through the lamp flame for purification; they then dip their fingers in the coloured powder and daub prayer marks on their foreheads. On Friday at around 11.30am, *prasada* (blessed vegetarian food) is offered to devotees.

Kukrit Pramoj Heritage House

Across Sathorn Road, the sprawling **Kukrit Pramoj Heritage House** at 19 Soi Phra Phinit (off Sathorn Tai Road; Sat–Sun 10am–5pm) is the former residence of the prolific author and statesman M.R. Kukrit Pramoj (1911–95). Educated at Oxford, he was the great-grandson of Rama II and uncle to Rama IX (the current king), and served as Thailand's prime minister in 1974 and 1975. Five traditional Thai teak houses occupy the main section of the compound, and behind them is a large garden decorated with Khmer stone art.

Patpong

Back on the northern side of Sathorn Road, the district known as **Patpong** ㉜, notorious for its go-go bars and sex shows, lies along two pedestrian-only lanes between Silom and Surawong roads. Patpong got its start as a convenient entertainment spot for international staff working at nearby airline offices in the late 1950s and early 1960s, and was further boosted by the arrival of US and Australian soldiers during the early 1970s Indochina War era. Patpong has slowly tamed itself over the years (much less total nudity nowadays, for example) and has transformed from a male-only enclave to a more general

Patpong Night Bazaar

tourist attraction. Although the neon-lit go-go action continues to this day, the **Patpong night bazaar** – rows of vendor carts hawking everything from cheap T-shirts to knock-off DVDs and fake designer watches in the middle of Patpong Soi 1 – has become an added draw.

EXCURSIONS FROM BANGKOK

When you've had enough of Bangkok's intensity, there are several spots outside the city you can escape to for a day or overnight. Within a 150km (93-mile) radius, you can choose among 16th- to 18th-century temple ruins in Ayutthaya, the tallest Buddhist monument in the world at Nakhon Pathom, the world-famous 'Bridge on the River Kwai' in Kanchanaburi and a park filled with scaled-down versions of historical architecture from all over the country. Closer is the river island of Ko Kret in Nonthaburi.

Ko Kret

An island in the middle of the Chao Phraya River in Non-thaburi, at Bangkok's northern edge, **Ko Kret** is home to one of Thailand's oldest Mon settlements. The Mon, who between the 6th and 10th centuries AD were the dominant culture in central Thailand, are skilled potters, and Ko Kret remains one of the oldest and largest sources of earthenware in the region. An exhibit of local pottery can be seen at the **Ancient Mon Pottery Centre**. You can also watch the locals crafting pottery.

Wat Porami Yikawat, known simply as Wat Mon, contains a Mon-style marble Buddha imported from Myanmar, a small museum and, at weekends, an outdoor market.

The easiest way to reach Ko Kret is by taxi to Pak Kret (around B200 from downtown, including expressway fees), then hop on a cross-river ferry to Ko Kret. Alternatively, the Chao Phraya River Express boat goes to Nonthaburi Pier, from where you can hire a longtail boat or taxi.

Ancient City (Muang Boran)

Covering over 120 hectares (300 acres), **Ancient City** ㉝ (Muang Boran; www.ancientcity.com; daily 9am–8pm) claims to be the largest open-air museum in the world. The outline of the complex mimics Thailand's geographical shape and encompasses 116 facsimiles of the kingdom's most famous monuments, along with related ponds, canals, gardens and linking walkways, offering a quick archaeological tour of the country. Monuments run the gamut from the stately temple ruins of Sukhothai in the north to the venerated Phra Boromathat *stupa* in Nakhon Si Thammarat in the south. Some are full-scale replicas, while others have been scaled down to one-third or three-quarters of the original. Wear comfortable shoes, as it takes a whole day to cover the huge area.

Ancient City has plenty of open space for picnics and leisurely walks. You can cover the complex in your car, by bicycle, golf cart or guided tram tour (charge for all). Snacks are available from boat vendors on the canals.

In the same area, **Samut Prakan Crocodile Farm and Zoo** (www.worldcrocodile.com; daily 8am–6pm) has over 30,000 crocodiles (including Yai, the largest croc in captivity at 1,115kg/2,450lbs), along with other animals. There are trained animal shows hourly, and feeding time is 4–5pm.

Ayutthaya

Thailand's royal capital from 1350 to 1767, the city of **Ayutthaya** ❸ is 86km (53 miles) north of Bangkok. It was named after Ayodhya (Sanskrit for 'unassailable' or 'undefeatable'), which is the home of Rama in the Indian epic *Ramayana*. City planners located the city at the confluence of the Chao Phraya, Pa Sak and Lopburi rivers, and added a wide canal to form a full circle of water around the town as a defence.

Samut Prakan Crocodile Farm and Zoo

Buddha head covered in banyan tree roots at Wat Mahathat

Ayutthaya's 400-year reign was Siam's historical apex, with sovereignty extending well into present-day Laos, Cambodia and Myanmar, and the kingdom's longest-enduring royal lineage (33 kings reigned before Ayutthaya was conquered by the Burmese in 1767). Thai culture and international commerce flourished, and the kingdom was courted by European, Chinese and Japanese merchants. By the end of the 17th century, Ayutthaya's population had reached 1 million – many foreign visitors recorded it to be the most illustrious city they had ever seen.

Today, Ayutthaya has preserved many of its Buddhist temple ruins, which together make up **Ayutthaya Historical Park**, a UNESCO World Heritage Site. Regular buses and trains to Ayutthaya leave Mo Chit bus terminal and Hualamphong station in Bangkok, but the most pleasant way to get here is by boat – several agencies offer day trips.

Although a modern city has encircled the ruin sites, Ayutthaya's historic temples are scattered throughout the island part of the city and along the encircling rivers and canal. Several of the more central ruins – **Wat Phra Si Sanphet**, **Wat Mongkhon Bophit**, **Wat Phra Ram**, **Wat Thammikarat**, **Wat Ratburana** and **Wat Mahathat** – can be visited on foot or rented bicycle. **Wat Phanan Choeng**, **Wat Phutthaisawan**, **Wat Kasatthirat** and **Wat Chai Wattanaram** are most conveniently toured by chartering a longtail boat.

Two museums, **Chao Sam Phraya National Museum** (Wed–Sun 9am–4pm) and **Chantharakasem National Museum** (Wed–Sun 9am–4pm; free) contain exhibits of Thai Buddhist art and archaeology, with an emphasis on the Ayutthaya period. The newer **Ayutthaya Historical Study Centre** (daily 9am-4pm) offers further insight into Ayutthaya's history with professionally curated displays focusing solely on the city.

Many visitors to Ayutthaya also visit **Bang Pa-In** (daily 8.30am–3.30pm), a summer palace complex built by Rama IV and his son Rama V, 20km (12 miles) to the south. The

Ayutthaya festivals

Ayutthaya holds one of the country's largest Loi Krathong festivals at the full moon of the 12th lunar month, usually November. Celebrations are held at several spots in Ayutthaya, with the largest spectacle taking place at Beung Phra Ram, a large lake in the centre of the city between Wat Phra Ram and Wat Mahathat. Tens of thousands of people, many from Bangkok, flock to the Beung Phra Ram event to crowd around five outdoor stages hosting *likay* (bawdy folk plays with dancing and music), Thai pop, outdoor cinema and *lakhon chaatree* (classical dance-drama). Food vendors and fireworks play a major part in the festivities. More low-key and traditional is the celebration at the Chan Kasem Pier, where families launch their *krathong* (small lotus-shaped floats made from banana leaves and topped with incense, flowers, coins and candles) onto the junction of the Lopburi and Pa Sak rivers. For a few baht you can be paddled out to the middle of the river to launch your own *krathong*.

Another major site for Loi Krathong is the Royal Folk Arts & Crafts Centre in Bang Sai, about 24km (15 miles) west of Ayutthaya. Here the emphasis is on traditional costumes and handmade *krathong*.

For 10 days in December, the Ayutthaya World Heritage Fair sees cultural performances and a sound-and-light show in the temple ruins.

Wat Phra Si Sanphet

most photographed feature of the complex is a pretty little Thai pavilion in a small lake by the entrance. Also of note are the Chinese-roofed **Wehat Chamrun Palace** and **Withun Thatsana** tower, which offers a fine view over the lakes and gardens, including a topiary with bushes trimmed to resemble a small herd of elephants.

Across the river and south from the palace grounds, **Wat Niwet Thamaprawat** is a Buddhist temple built by Rama V in 1878 in the style of a Christian church, complete with stained-glass windows and Gothic spires.

Phra Pathom Chedi

Nakhon Pathom ㉟ (population 50,000), 56km (35 miles) west of Bangkok, is often called the oldest city in Thailand, and its name in fact means 'First City'. It may once have served as the power centre for the Dvaravati kingdom, a collection of Mon city-states that flourished between the 6th and 11th centuries

AD. The town's world-famous **Phra Pathom Chedi**, at 127m (417ft) the tallest Buddhist monument in the world, is said to encase a 6th-century *stupa* within its huge ochre-glazed dome.

In the early 11th century, Khmer king Suryavarman I conquered Nakhon Pathom and built an Angkor-style tower over the Mon *stupa*. After Burmese armies sacked the city in 1057, the tower lay in ruins until Rama IV restored the monument in 1860, building the current larger *stupa* over the remains. A **national museum** (Wed–Sun 9am–4pm) contains displays of Dvaravati-era sculpture and other artefacts.

Floating markets

Several **floating markets** ❸ can be visited along canals to the southwest of Bangkok in Samut Songkhram and Ratchaburi provinces. **Ton Khem Floating Market**, a century-old market on Damnoen Saduak Canal around 100km (62 miles) southwest of Bangkok, is the largest, while **Hia Kui Floating Market**, just south of Damnoen Saduak on parallel Hia Kui Canal, is the most popular with visitors. A third, somewhat less crowded market can be found on nearby Khun Phitak Canal at **Khun Phitak Floating Market**. Boats can be rented to tour the canals and all three markets. Try to arrive by 8am at the latest, as by 9am the markets are very crowded.

Around 7km (4 miles) northwest of Samut Songkhram, **Amphawa Floating Market** (Fri–Sun noon–9pm) operates weekend evenings in front of Wat Amphawa. It's best to get there from 3pm by which time all the stalls are operating.

Phra Pathom Chedi

Boats loaded with fruits and vegetables in Amphawa
Floating Market

Kanchanaburi

Around 130km (80 miles) west of Bangkok, in the slightly elevated Mae Klong River valley, **Kanchanaburi** ③⑦ is surrounded by hills and sugar-cane plantations. Rama I originally established the town as a first line of defence against the Burmese who might invade via Three Pagodas Pass on the Thai-Burmese border.

During World War II, the Japanese built the infamous Death Railway along this same invasion route, in reverse, along the Khwae Noi River, using Allied prisoners of war and Southeast Asian draft labourers. Thousands died as a result of brutal treatment by their captors, a story chronicled by Pierre Boulle's *The Bridge on the River Kwai*, which was made into an Oscar-winning film of the same name (1957) by David Lean.

The steel **Death Railway Bridge** (famously known as 'the bridge on the River Kwai') still spans the Khwae Yai River, a tributary of the Mae Klong, 3km (nearly 2 miles) from the centre of town. The strategic objective of the railway was to secure an alternative supply route for the Japanese conquest of Burma (Myanmar) and other Asian countries to the west. The materials for the bridge were brought from Java by the Imperial Japanese Army during their occupation of Thailand. The first version of the bridge, completed in February 1943, was all wood. In 1945, the bridge was bombed several times and was only rebuilt after the war – the curved portions of the bridge are original. An estimated 16,000 prisoners of war died while building the 415km (258-mile), narrow-gauge Death Railway to Burma, roughly two-thirds of which ran through Thailand. Death rates of labourers from Thailand, Burma, Malaysia and Indonesia were even higher: 90,000 to 100,000 in 16 months.

The best place to start your exploration of the Kanchanaburi area is at the **Thailand-Burma Railway Centre** (www.tbrc online.com; daily 9am–5pm), where you can walk through eight galleries of displays chronicling the history of the railway and Japanese aggression in Southeast Asia during World War II.

Opposite the museum, the **Kanchanaburi Allied War Cemetery** (also known as Don-Rak War Cemetery; daily 7am–6pm; free) is where 6,982 Australian, Dutch and British prisoners of war who lost their lives during the construction of Death Railway are buried or commemorated. Lovingly tended, the cemetery is a touching gift from the Thai people to the countries whose citizens died on their soil. The less visited **Chung Kai Allied War Cemetery** commemorates more soldiers.

Best and most moving of all is the smaller **JEATH**

The deadly bridge

In normal times, a 415km (258-mile) rail line through difficult terrain would have taken five years to complete, but in World War II, the Japanese forced the POWs and coolies to complete it in 16 months. The Japanese used the infamous bridge for only 20 months before it was bombed by the Allies in 1945.

War Museum (daily 8.30am–6pm), which occupies a portion of the grounds of Wat Chaichumphon and displays replicas of the bamboo huts used to shelter prisoners of war. Inside the the huts are war-era photos, drawings and paintings by the prisoners, weapons and other war memorabilia. JEATH stands for Japan, England, Australia/America, Thailand and Holland, the six countries who were embroiled at Kanchanaburi during World War II.

Kanchanaburi District is also famous for its cave temples. At **Wat Tham Mongkon Thong**, dragon-banister stairs ascend a steep slope to reach a complex of limestone caves filled with Buddha images and other sacred sculptures. Every Sunday a white-robed Thai Buddhist nun displays Buddha-like hand gestures while floating on her back in a round water tank, a devotional exhibition known to tour guides as the 'floating nun'. Devotees from all over Thailand come to watch the ritual and to receive the nun's blessings.

Two larger cave monasteries, Wat Tham Seua and Wat Tham Khao Noi, sprawl across a mountain ridge 15km (9 miles) southeast of Kanchanaburi. **Wat Tham Seua**'s dominating feature is a large seated Buddha overlooking the Mae Klong River. An alms bowl in the figure's lap receives money offerings sent to it via a hand-operated conveyor belt. Steps to the right of the monastery's main entry stairs lead up to an aviary harbouring a variety of tropical birdlife and to a cave that is filled with Buddhas.

The Chinese temple architecture of **Wat Tham Khao Noi** is inspired by Penang's Kek Lok Si. A stroll to the top of the complex yields some impressive views of the Khwae River and agricultural fields.

Escape to Ko Samet

Sunthon Phu's *Phra Aphaimani* follows the travails of a prince exiled to an undersea kingdom ruled by a lovesick female giant. A mermaid aids the prince in his escape to Ko Samet, where he defeats the giant by playing a magic flute.

Ko Samet

This T-shaped island to the southeast of Bangkok is well known to students of Thai literature as a setting for the classical epic *Phra Aphaimani* by Sunthon Phu. In Thailand's 1980s economic boom, the 13-sq km (5-sq mile) island began receiving its first visitors, who were more interested in sand and sea than in literature, as young Bangkokians made it a popular weekend retreat. Although the northeastern coast is crowded with inexpensive resorts, the white sand beaches become gradually less busy towards the central and southern shores.

Ko Samet's idyllic beaches

To get to **Ko Samet** 🟠, take the public bus from Ekamai Bus Station in Bangkok to Ban Phe pier. The boat journey from Ban Phe to Ko Samet takes about 45 minutes. Parts of the island come under the jurisdiction of Laem Ya–Ko Samet National Marine Park, and all visitors must pay a fee on arrival. The park's main office is near Hat Sai Kaew, a smaller one is at Ao Wong Deuan. During Thailand's annual southwest monsoon (June–Nov), Ko Samet's east coast is shielded from the heavier rains, so it is popular all year round. Ko Samet can be especially busy during Thai public holidays.

Boat tours around Ko Samet and neighbouring islands, including to the Turtle Conservation Centre on Ko Man Nai, are popular. Snorkelling and diving excursions can also be taken.

WHAT TO DO

SHOPPING

In terms of sheer variety and value, Bangkok offers some of Asia's best shopping experiences. From the cramped vendor stalls of local markets to the chic boutiques of Southeast Asia's largest super-mall, you will easily find enough shopping options to keep you busy from dawn to midnight.

Markets

Chatuchak Weekend Market (Sat–Sun 8am–6pm), in the northern part of the city adjacent to Chatuchak Park, is the granddaddy of all Bangkok markets, a conglomeration of over 8,000 stalls purveying practically everything that can be legally sold in Thailand. This market Disneyland is a particularly good hunting ground for second-hand books, design accessories, handicrafts, beads, Thai music CDs, religious amulets, clothing from India and Nepal, military surplus gear and household goods. Bargaining is definitely the order of the day. If hunger strikes, there are plenty of inexpensive but high-quality Thai restaurants. Arrive as early in the morning as possible to avoid the crowds and heat.

Take the ten-minute shuttle boat from Saphan Taksin pier to reach Asiatique (daily 5pm–midnight; www.thaiasiatique. com) a market that is also one of Bangkok's few pedestrian-friendly waterfront spaces. The stalls include handicrafts, home decor and clothes; there are also waterfront restaurants and several theatre shows.

Bangkok's infamous backpacker centre, **Khao San Road**, has developed a bustling street market during its lengthy reign

Chatuchak Weekend Market

as Asia's most popular travel stopover. During the day, vendors are confined to the pavements on either side of the road, but at night, when Khao San Road is closed to vehicles, they spill into the street, along with *phat thai* (fried rice noodles) carts and VW vans converted into cocktail bars. Dreadlocked merchants specialise in inexpensive beach and travel clothing, luggage and travel accessories, costume jewellery, original-design T-shirts, pirate CDs and DVDs and hair extensions.

A more dense array of market stalls line the two parallel roads of **Patpong** (daily 5pm–midnight), more famous for its go-go bars, massage parlours and sex shows. Here the selection confines itself to tourist clothing, fake designer watches and handbags, pirate CDs and DVDs (both porn and non-porn) and mainstream Thai souvenirs. Not far away, **Soi Lalai Sap**, the 'money-melting soi' at Soi 5, Silom Road, is a favourite after-lunch stop for local office workers shopping for inexpensive clothing, watches, electronics and housewares.

The **Pahurat** and **Chinatown** districts have interconnected lanes lined with hundreds of vendors selling well-priced Thai, Indian and Chinese fabrics, along with clothes and accessories, gems and jewellery. The **Wong Wian Yai Market** in Thonburi, next to the large roundabout directly southwest of Memorial Bridge, is another all-purpose market, and one that rarely sees tourists.

Spreading over several blocks along Chakraphong, Phra Sumen, Tanao and Rambutri roads, not far from Khao San Road, **Banglamphu Market** is one of the city's

---

Traditional cures

Elsewhere along Maharat Road near Wat Mahathat are several traditional Thai medicine shops. The proprietors offer both commercially prepared and custom-blended medicines, most made from natural herbs and plants following age-old Thai and Chinese recipes. Aromatic massage oils are also available, and a few of the shops offer traditional Thai massage.

most comprehensive shopping districts, as it encompasses everything from street vendors to budget department stores. The area offers better-than-average value on clothing, foodstuffs (including packaged Thai curry pastes) and household items, but there is not much to be found in the way of souvenirs and handicrafts.

The **Maharat Amulet Market** (daily 8am–6pm), occupying several narrow lanes off Maharat Road, opposite Wat Mahathat, offers row upon row of large glass cases filled with sacred amulets (*phra khreuang* in Thai). Each flat piece – usually triangle-shaped – is imprinted with

Amulets for sale

an image of the Buddha, Ganesha, a highly venerated Buddhist monk, or other holy entity. Depending on the amulet and its provenance, the images are said to offer protection against accident and injury, or to further one's career or personal charisma. Prices range from as little as 50 baht for ordinary amulets to tens of thousands of baht for those that are thought to have strong magical powers. Full-size standing and seated Buddha images are also for sale here. Another amulet market can be found at **Wat Ratchanatda**, which is near Mahakan Fort.

Shopping centres and department stores

In Bangkok you can barely travel more than half a kilometre without passing a shopping centre or department store. Many

Shopping in Siam Square

are concentrated along Rama I, Ploenchit and Sukhumvit roads, starting from the area around Siam Square.

MBK (Mahboonkrong) Centre (www.mbk-center.co.th), across from Siam Discovery Centre, is one of the capital's most varied and affordable shopping venues. Anchored by the middle-class **Tokyu** department store, MBK packs in hundreds of small shops and hallway vendor stalls selling bargain-priced clothing, photographic equipment and consumer electronics, along with perhaps the largest selection of mobile (cell) phones in Bangkok.

Siam Square, across Phaya Thai Road from MBK, is made up of 12 *soi* (lanes) that are lined with new malls and shops offering books, sporting goods, casual clothing and antiques, along with a branch of Bangkok Bank, several money-exchange booths, travel agencies, cinemas and restaurants. Tucked away in sub-*sois* are small shops owned and operated by up-and-coming local designers. Their ready-to-wear clothes often reflect the latest world fashion trends, but tagged with bargain-basement prices.

Diagonally opposite MBK, on Rama I Road, **Siam Discovery** (www.siamdiscovery.co.th) has designer and home interior shops; on the top floor there's an ice rink, the Grand EGV cinema and Madame Tussaud's waxworks museum. Next door, **Siam Centre** (www.siamcenter.co.th) was Thailand's first shopping mall when it was built on crown property in 1976. Completely refurbished in 2013, its funky new interior harbours designer and brand-label clothing stores, as well as boutique opticians, coffee shops and restaurants.

Siam Paragon (www.siamparagon.co.th), one of Southeast Asia's largest malls, corrals half a million square metres of potential purchases. State-of-the-art boutiques stock the latest designer fashions, home furnishings and consumer electronics, while the mall's own **Paragon Department Store** occupies parts of several floors. Gourmet food centres abound, and entertainment options include the Siam Paragon IMAX and Cineplex and Siam Ocean World Aquarium.

From Paragon there starts a series of malls owned by Central Group, beginning with **Central World** (www.centralworld.co.th), which at 800,000 sq m (957,000 sq yds) is Bangkok's biggest shopping mall. It is filled with a melange of fashion, sports, electronics, toys, cosmetics and restaurants. An outdoor beer garden with live shows in the cool season is a major location for Bangkok's New Year Countdown.

On the opposite corner is **Gaysorn Plaza** (www.gaysorn.com), a good place for modern Thai design shops, and beyond is **Central Department Store** (www.central.co.th). In addition to designer clothing, Western cosmetics, fabrics, furniture, handicrafts and attached supermarket, the store offers free alteration on all clothing purchases and free delivery to Bangkok hotels. There's also a fix-it area for watch, shoe and clothing repair. Central's lower-priced subsidiary, **Robinsons**, also has branches throughout the city.

Another 100 metres/yards brings you to the luxury-branded Central Embassy (www.centralembassy.com), opened in 2014 on former British Embassy land.

Other convenient stops are **Terminal 21** (beside Asoke BTS station; www.terminal21.co.th), and **Emporium Shopping Centre** (beside Phrom Phong; www.emporiumthailand.com), which is noteworthy for many European and Thai designer clothing boutiques, interior design shops, an upmarket food centre, Kinokuniya bookshop and a cineplex.

River City Complex (www.rivercity.co.th), a four-storey shopping centre on the Chao Phraya River next to the Royal

Thai tailors

Bangkok's many tailor shops can design, cut and sew shirts, dresses, trousers, suits and just about any other article of clothing. Workmanship ranges from shoddy to excellent, so shop around. Most single-piece items, such as a jacket, simple dress, shirt or trousers, can be finished in 48 hours or less with only one fitting. For something more complicated like a suit, the more reputable tailors will ask for two to five sittings.

Bangkok tailors are also adept at copying examples provided by their customers, whether from the original item or a photo. Custom-made shirts or dresses can be knocked off for not much more than a tenth of the designer price.

Thai and Chinese silks are a popular and reasonably priced choice of fabric. Most of the 'cotton' offered by Bangkok tailors is actually a blend of cotton and a synthetic, so bring your own if you want to be assured of 100 percent cotton. 'Special deals' advertising four shirts, two suits, a kimono and a safari suit all in one package almost always turn out to be of inferior materials and workmanship.

Orchid Sheraton, has quality art and antique shops on the third and fourth floors.

Silom Village Trade Centre (www.silomvillage.co.th) on Silom Road, contains less expensive shops selling art, antiques and handicrafts. Here Artisan's specialises in reproduction antique Thai furniture made from recycled teak.

Buy books at Siam Paragon shopping mall

Bangkok is home to leading coloured gem cutters, and many shops cluster around the **Jewellery Trade Centre** (919/1 Silom Road; www.jewelrytradecenter.com; daily 10am-8pm), where you can have gemstones graded at the **Asian Institute of Gemological Sciences** (www.aigsthailand.com; Mon–Fri 8am–6pm).

Books

Bangkok offers one of the best selections of English-language books and bookshops in Southeast Asia. **Asia Books** (Siam Paragon; Central World; Terminal 21; Sukhumvit Road near Soi 15; Emporium) has branches sprinkled around Central Bangkok and **Kinokuniya** (Siam Paragon; Emporium) has the best selection in the city.

Dasa Book Café (between Sukhumvit Soi 26 and 28; www.dasabookcafe.com) has second-hand books in a cosy environment with drinks and desserts to fuel your page thumbing. They even have an online database, so you don't have to waste your time looking for something that is not there. Backpackers ensure a good turnover of titles at several stalls and shops in the Khao San Road area.

Antiques

Genuine Thai antiques are rare and costly, and most Bangkok antique shops nowadays supplement their collection of coveted Thai pieces with antiques from neighbouring Myanmar, Laos and China, along with traditionally crafted items made to resemble antiques. The majority of shop operators are candid about what's truly old and what isn't. Good buys include Thai-style furniture made with old teak salvaged from abandoned homes and rice barns. Note that antique Buddha images may not be taken out of the country, and even new images (other than amulets) require a permit from the Department of Fine Arts (tel: 0 2226 1661).

ENTERTAINMENT

In their round-the-clock search for *sanuk* (fun), Bangkokians have made their metropolis one that virtually never sleeps. For an idea of what's on, check the daily entertainment listings in the *Bangkok Post* and *The Nation*. For dance club and live music information log on to BK Magazine (www.bkmagazine.com) or Siam2Nite (www.siam2nite.com).

Theatre

Known in Thai as Sala Chalerm Krung, the **Chalermkrung Royal Theatre** (Old Siam Plaza, corner of Charoen Krung and Triphet roads; tel: 0-2222 0434) is one of Bangkok's top venues for *khon* (classical masked dance-drama). The 1933 Thai Deco cinema has a 170-member dance troupe that combines superb costuming, set design, dancing and music. Performances are usually on Thursdays and Fridays and last two hours with an interval.

The newer **Siam Niramit Theatre** (Tiam Ruammit Road, opposite the Thailand Cultural Centre; tel: 0-2649 9222;

www.siamniramit.com) presents a more technologically enhanced version of *khon* on a huge stage, using laser-based special effects; more than 150 performers run through up to 500 costumes.

Aksra Theatre (8/1 Soi Rangnam; www.aksratheatre.com) mixes Thai and other Asian puppetry with cultural performances and mainstream popular theatre.

Tawandang German Brewery (462/61 Thanon Rama III; www.tawandang.com) is a huge pub-cum-theatre with traditional and modern Thai music, costumed dancers and sometimes even magic acts.

Scene from the Sala Rim Naam dance show at the Mandarin Oriental hotel

The **Joe Louis Theatre** (Asiatique, Charoen Krung Sois 72-76, tel: 0-2108 4488; www.joelouistheatre.com) has nightly shows of traditional Thai puppetry at 8pm. Another option at Asiatique is **Calypso** (www.calypsocabaret.com), for Vegas-style lip-synching shows performed by transsexuals, who are known as 'lady-boys' or *kathoeys*.

Bars

The curved **Sky Bar** (Lebua, Silom Rd; www.lebua.com) has an unparalleled nightscape, perched 63 floors high above the city in the outdoor Sirocco restaurant. It is among several rooftop bars and restaurants in Bangkok.

The outdoor terrace at Sirocco

One of the city's classiest watering holes, **Maggie Choo's** (320. Silom Rd; 0-2635 6055; www.facebook.com/maggiechoos) is a fantasy 1930s' Shanghai bordello disguised as a bank, complete with busts of Queen Victoria, live bands and performers in slit-to-the-thigh Chinese dresses. Other funky bars include **Oskar** (Sukhumvit Soi 11; www.facebook.com/OskarBangkok) and **Iron Fairies** (Soi Thonglor; www.facebook.com/ironfairies bkk). At the no-frills end of the scale try **Cheap Charlie's**, which is literally just a bar (no walls), or vendors selling alcohol from the backs of camper vans, both on Soi 11.

Taverns and sports bars serving draught beer and pub grub include **The Robin Hood** (cnr Sukhumvit 33/1; www.therobinhoodbangkok.com) and **Molly Malone's** (Soi Convent; www.mollymalonesbangkok.com). Amid the packed Khao San area, a cooler scene happens along Phra Artht Road at bars like **Dickinson's**.

Dance clubs

Sukhumvit Soi 11 is among several hot spots where local and international DJs spin everything from house to hip-hop, with bangra beats in between. **Q Bar** (www.qbarbangkok.com) also has a cute absinthe bar at the back, while **Bash** (www.bashbangkok.com) stays open way past bedtime. There's more action on Soi Thonglor, where **Demo** (Thonglor Soi 10; www.

facebook.com/demobangkok) attracts crowds with mock classical French furniture and graffiti covered walls in an urban warehouse setting.

In the Silom area, the Singapore nightlife brand **Ku De Ta** (www.kudeta.com) opened beside Chong Nonsi Skytrain station in 2013, bringing multiple sophisticated venues, a cutting edge sound system and spectacular views. The gay scene is vibrant on Silom Sois 2 and 4, with **DJ Station** (www.dj-station.com) being particularly popular.

Over on Khao San Road, young Thais and foreign backpackers gather at **The Club** (www.theclubkhaosan.com) for house, techno and electro beats in a fairytale castle interior with occasional live musicians and pro dancers.

Go-go bars

Prostitution may be illegal in Thailand, but Bangkok's world-famous red-light scene is highly visible in four main areas of the city. The oldest and most well-known, Patpong (named after its billionaire Thai-Chinese owner), consists of two adjacent pedestrian-only lanes between Silom and Surawong roads and lined with bright neon signs advertising go-go bars and 'live shows'. Stalls selling cheap souvenirs and fake designer goods fill the centre of Patpong 2 at night. Nearby Soi Pratuchai and Soi Anuman Ratchathon feature similarly themed bars directed towards gay males.

Soi Cowboy, between Soi 21 and Soi 23, Sukhumvit Road, offers a strip of go-go bars. Not far away on Soi 4, Sukhumvit Road, Nana Entertainment Plaza crams go-go bars into a U-shaped, three-storey complex.

A fourth area, Ratchada, along four-lane Ratchadaphisek Road in the Huay Khwang district in northeast Bangkok, mostly caters to a visiting Japanese and Chinese clientele with mega-large entertainment centres containing massage parlours, hostess bars and karaoke lounges.

Live music

Bangkok's regular live music scene ebbs and flows around a number of venues and genres, and many international acts visit for concerts large and small. **Saxophone Pub** (3/8 Victory Monument, Phayathai Road; www.saxophonepub. com), just off the Victory Monument roundabout, offers a schedule that alternates nightly between blues, jazz and R&B.

The city has several jazz faculties. Good places to check out local talent, include **Brown Sugar** (Phra Sumen Rd; www. brownsugarbangkok.com) and Jazz Happens (Phra Arthit Rd), both located in the Khao San area.

Imported musicians take the stage at the city's most elegant jazz club, The Oriental's legendary **Bamboo Bar**, where visiting jazz singers front the house jazz band. The Sheraton Grand's **Living Room** is another hotel lounge hosting top class jazz musicians.

In northern Banglamphu, the cryptically named **Ad Here the 13th** (13 Samsen Road, near Soi 1) features some of the capital's most authentic blues playing in a long, narrow bar with a steady Thai and expat following.

The **Brick Bar** in the basement of the Buddy Lodge on Khao San Road has a varied program of live acts attracting a mostly Thai crowd.

Metal bands and various sub genres shake the walls of **The Rock Pub** on Phaya Thai Road (www.therock pub-bangkok.com), while indie outfits play irregular

Late-night venues

Officially, Bangkok's nightlife has three zones: Silom, Ratchadaphisek and Royal City Avenue (RCA), where venues with dance licences can open until 2am. The rest should close by 1am. Actual times depend more often on the bar paying the right people under the table, so late night parties are never far away. The requirement to be over-20 to enter clubs is more strictly enforced. Almost all require you to show ID.

Party time at Q Bar

events at cosy venues such as **Moonstar Studios**. Classical concerts occur monthly at **Sala Sudasiri Sobha** (158/20 Ladprao 41; www.salasudasirisobha.com) and there are several lavish productions each year from Bangkok Opera. Check out **Thai Ticketmajor** (www.thaiticketmajor.com) and **Siam2Nite** (www.siam2nite.com) for updates on acts of all types.

Cinema

Multiplex cinemas showing Thai films and the latest block-busters can be found in nearly every neighbourhood. The highest concentration of cinemas, and those with the best sound systems and most comfortable seating, is in Central Bangkok near Siam Square, in Siam Paragon and the MBK Centre. **EGV**, **Major** and **SF** are the top chains. **House** (UMG Cinema, RCA, Rama IX Road, www.houserama.com) special-ises in independent films.

SPORT

Muay Thai

Thailand's national sport, the ancient art of Thai kickboxing (*muay thai*), is practised at several government-owned stadiums in and around Bangkok. Most centrally located is **Ratchadamnoen Boxing Stadium** (Ratchadamnoen Nok Road, next to the TAT information office). Bangkok's other major venue, **Lumpinee Boxing Stadium** (6 Ramintra Rd; www.muaythailumpinee.net) is now in the north of the city. The typical fight roster presents eight fights of five rounds each. Admission fees vary according to seating. Ratchadamnoen fights take place on Monday, Wednesday and Thursday from 6.30pm, and on Sunday from 5pm. Lumpinee bouts are held Tuesday and Friday from 6.30pm, and on Saturday from 5pm. The best matches are reserved for Thursday nights at Ratchadamnoen and Tuesday nights at Lumpinee.

You can also train at several gyms around the city, such as **Sor Vorapin** (13 Trok Kasab; www.thaiboxings.com), near Khao San Road.

Takraw

In *takraw* several players stand in a circle (the size of the circle depends on the number of players) and try to keep a 12cm (5in) rattan ball aloft by kicking it from one player to another, earning points for style and technique. A more modern variation uses a volleyball court, and is played much like volleyball (with only the feet and head allowed to touch the ball). In yet another variation, players kick the ball into a loosely woven hoop suspended 4.5m (15ft) above the ground. Regular matches are held at the **National Stadium** (Rama I Road), in **Lumpini Park** and on school grounds and university campuses throughout the city.

A game of takraw

Other sports

In Thailand **golf** is a sport for the wealthy, and with so much wealth concentrated in Bangkok, there are plenty of well-groomed 18-hole golf courses around the city in adjacent provinces such as Pathum Thani and Chonburi. Most provide transport (at additional cost) from Bangkok with a reserved tee-off. One popular option is **Bangkok Golf Club** (99 Moo 2 Thanon Tivanond; tel: 0-2501 2828; www.golf.th.com), which is only 40 minutes from central Bangkok and has a nine-hole par three course along with the full 18 holes. Others include the **President Country Club** (42 Mu 8, Suwinthawong Road, Nong Chok, tel: 0-2988 7555, www.president.co.th) and the **Thai Country Country Club** (88 Moo 1, Bangna-Trad Km. 35.5; tel: 0-2651 5300; www.thaicountryclub.com).

Tennis courts open to the public include **Santisuk Tennis Courts** (Sukhumvit Road between Soi 36 and Soi 38). There's also Bowling at **SF Strike Bowl** (7th Floor MBK; tel: 0-2611

Sea life at Siam Ocean World

7171; www.sfcinemacity. com), Karting at **EasyKart** (2nd Floor, RCA Plaza, Royal City Avenue, Rama IX Rd; tel: 08-9072 7447; www.easykart. net) and Flowboarding, a cross between snowboarding, skateboarding and surfing, at **Flow House Bangkok** (A Square, Sukhumvit Soi 26; tel: 0-2108 5210, www.flow housebangkok.com).

Horse racing takes place at **Royal Turf Club of Thailand** (Phitsanulok Road; tel: 0-2280 0020) and **Royal Bangkok Sports Club** (Henri Dunant Road; tel: 0-2251 0181) on alternate Sundays, 12.30am–6pm.

CHILDREN'S BANGKOK

Bangkok has plenty of activities for children. For a start there is the Dusit Zoo, Snake Farm, Lumpini Park and Samut Prakan Crocodile Farm and Zoo.

Siam Ocean World (Siam Paragon, Rama I Road; tel: 0-2610 9000; www.siamoceanworld.com; daily 9am–10pm) is South East Asia's largest oceanarium with huge numbers of ocean dwelling species including sharks and penguins.

Outside central Bangkok Safari World (99 Panyaintra Road; tel: 0-2914 4100; www.safariworld.com; daily 9am–5pm) has safari and marine parks, and **Siam Park** (99 Seri Thai Road, Kanna Yao; daily 10am–6pm; tel: 0-2919 7200; www.siampark city.com) has a water park with wave pools, a bird park with aviaries, plus a children's playground, and botanical gardens.

Calendar of events

Dates for Buddhist festivals vary from year to year in accordance with Thailand's traditional lunar calendar.

January–February *Chinese New Year* (date varies from year to year): Chinatown brings in the new year with lion dances and fireworks.

February–March *Magha Puja* (full moon of the third lunar month): commemoration of an apocryphal tale in 1250 when monks turned up to hear the Buddha preach without a prior announcement. A candlelit walk to the summit of the Golden Mount is a highlight.

13–15 April *Songkhran Festival*: Thailand's traditional new year celebration involves pouring water over an image of the Buddha and over monks and community elders. In the streets, Thais throw water from bowls or buckets onto passers-by during the daytime; once night falls, everything returns to normal.

May *Visakha Puja* (15th day of the waxing moon in the sixth lunar month): this important day celebrates the Buddha's birth, enlightenment and *parinibbana*; candlelit processions and chanting in Buddhist monasteries. *Royal Ploughing Ceremony*: an ancient Brahmanic ritual, in which rice seed is ceremonially sowed at Sanam Luang just before the rainy season to bring good rains to farmers; the king presides over the ceremony, which attracts thousands of Thais.

July *Asalha Puja*: a day honouring the Buddha's first sermon; Theravada Buddhist temples in the capital host hold candlelit processions.

September–October *Vegetarian Festival* (first nine days of ninth lunar month): an orgy of vegetarian food in Chinatown for nine days.

November *Loi Krathong* (full moon of the 12th lunar month): small lotus-shaped floats are loaded with flowers, incense, candles and a coin, and then launched on Bangkok's rivers and canals.

3 December *Trooping of the Colour*, outside the old Thai Parliament, when the royal family review the elite Royal Guard, who are clad in brightly coloured dress uniforms.

5 December *King's Birthday*: celebrations include an elaborate parade on Ratchadamnoen Klang Avenue.

EATING OUT

Bangkok lures more visitors than any other capital in Southeast Asia not only because of its spectacular temples and renowned nightlife, but also because it offers one of the most robust and varied cuisines in the region. Whether following carefully preserved royal Thai recipes or inspired by the latest Mediterranean fusion cooking techniques, Bangkok's cooks can collectively boast a vast arsenal of tongue-tempting delights.

WHERE TO EAT

You can't walk more than a few metres in the capital without coming across a street stall, a cluster of tables on the pavement, or a restaurant. Most dining venues in Bangkok's tourist districts offer menus in English, but in places where there are no English menus there's usually someone who can help you order. Many restaurants have their own house specialities in addition to what's listed on the menu, so it's worth asking the waiter for recommendations.

Economical places to eat include noodle shops (*raan kuaytiaw*), curry-rice shops (*raan khao kaeng*), food centres (*suun aahaan*) and night markets (*talaat toh rung*). In addition to being inexpensive, the dishes served at such places are invariably delicious and very authentic. Some of the best and cheapest food can be found at

> ### Budget grub
>
> Backpackers can find plenty to please both the palate and the pocket on and around Khao San Road in Banglamphu. Night markets such as the Soi 38 Night Market (Soi 38, Sukhumvit Road) and Suan Luang Night Market (Soi 5, Ban That Thong, near Chulalongkorn University) feature cheap yet marvellously authentic Thai dishes.

food stalls lining the streets. Vendors buy their ingredients fresh from the market in the early morning and prepare their dishes before your very eyes.

At a curry-rice shop *(raan khao kaeng)*, pots of curry will be placed on a table towards the front of the shop, along with a large rice cooker. Curry-rice shops open early in the morning and usually close by 2pm.

At the other end of the scale, the arrival of bo.lan restaurant in 2009 heralded a new wave of superb upmarket restaurants that provide traditional Thai flavours, as opposed to the milder

A tasty Massaman curry

tourist-oriented fare that until then was more often found in upscale restaurants. Some exciting modern Thai places have begun opening, following in the wake of Sra Bua, launched in 2010. Fine dining is also found in luxury hotels such as The Metropolitan and The Four Seasons, and Joel Robuchon is due to open an outlet by 2015.

International dining options in Bangkok are rich and varied, with every major Asian and Western cuisine well covered. Chinese food is naturally best in Bangkok's **Chinatown**, Indian food in the Indian-dominated neighbourhoods of **Phahurat** and **Bangrak**, and Middle Eastern in the **Nana** neighbourhood off Sukhumvit Road. Sukhumvit is also your best bet for Italian and French cuisines.

WHAT TO EAT

Thai cooking

Bangkok cuisine relies heavily on fresh ingredients. Fresh vegetables, poultry, pork and beef are the main ingredients, usually cooked quickly by stir-frying, steaming or parboiling. Fresh lime juice, kaffir lime leaves, lemongrass and coriander leaf are added to give the food its characteristic tang, while fish sauce (*naam plaa*) or shrimp paste (*ka-pi*) contribute salty tones.

Three members of the ginger family – galangal (*khaa*), ginger (*khing*) and turmeric (*kha-min*) – also find their way into many dishes. In addition, cooks season the food with black pepper, three kinds of basil, ground peanuts (more often a condiment), tamarind juice and coconut milk.

Some Thai dishes can be very spicy, particularly those containing fresh *phrik khee nuu*, small torpedo-shaped bird chillies

Eating Thai-style

Most Thai dishes are eaten with a fork (*sawm*) and tablespoon (*chawn*). Proper etiquette dictates that you eat with the spoon, the fork being used only to prod the food onto the spoon. Chopsticks (*ta-kiap*) are used only when eating in Chinese restaurants or for eating noodle dishes.

Thai meals are shared among the diners and served from common serving platters in the centre of the table. When taking food from a common platter, you place only one spoonful at a time onto your plate.

Typically the table orders one of each kind of dish, for example, one spicy dish, one mild dish, one fish dish, one soup and so on. One or two extra dishes will be ordered when there are four or more diners.

Many restaurants will have a separate *jaan diaw* (one-plate dish) section on the menu listing rice and noodle dishes. Solo diners can also order dishes over rice (*raat khao*).

which timid eaters may want to push aside. Less spicy dishes use dried chilli flakes and a few contain no chillies at all.

Rice *(khao)* is eaten with most meals, and in fact the Thai phrase 'to eat' is *kin khao*, literally 'eat rice'. There are many varieties and grades of rice, with the finest known as *khao hawm mali* or 'jasmine-scented rice' for its sweet, inviting smell when cooked.

Preparing street food on Khao San Road

Combining coconut cream, fresh-pounded chillies, ginger, garlic and onions, Thai curries *(kaeng)* are among the hottest in the world. They come in several varieties, including red curry *(kaeng phet)*, green curry *(kaeng khiaw-waan)* and mild peanut-based curry *(kaeng phanaeng)*. Most fiery of all is the 'jungle curry' *(kaeng paa)*, which dispenses with the coconut cream for a pure chilli base.

Stir-fried dishes are the most popular choice among Bangkokians. Favourites include *phat bai ka-phrao* (chicken or pork stir-fried with basil, garlic, fresh chilli and soy sauce), *kai phat phrik khing* (chicken stir-fried with ginger and dried red chilli) and *kai phat met ma-muang himaphaan* (sliced chicken stir-fried with cashews and dried chilli).

Another Thai staple is *yam*, a hot, tangy salad made with a mixture of fresh and cooked ingredients. One of the most common is *yam plaa duk fuu*, which tosses together fried grated catfish, fresh chopped chilli and peanuts, served with a spicy/salty/sour green mango dressing on the side.

Two of the most common Thai soups are fiery *tom yam* (spicy lemongrass soup, usually made with seafood) and less spicy *tom kha* (spicy coconut cream and galangal soup, usually

Literally high-end dining at Vertigo Restaurant

served with filleted chicken). They are served with steamed rice to soak up the excess chilli heat.

Smaller dishes meant to be eaten while drinking alcoholic beverages are called *kap klaem*. Some Thai menus translate these as 'snacks' or 'appetisers'. Typical *kap klaem* include fried peanuts *(thua thawt)* and spicy cashew salad *(yam met ma-muang himaphaan)*.

Noodles come in two basic varieties, white rice noodles *(kuaytiaw)* and yellow wheat noodles *(ba-mee)*. Either can be ordered in a soup *(naam)*, or as steamed noodles without broth *(haeng)* or stir-fried *(phat)* with other ingredients. One can choose between several meats, most commonly chicken, pork and beef, with seafood an occasional option.

Thais rarely order desserts or pastries at the end of a meal, but rather freshly sliced fruit. Pineapple, papaya, watermelon, mandarin orange, guava, mango and banana are the most commonly served fruits, but diners may also come across starfruit and pomelo. The infamous durian – known as the 'king of fruits' for its rich and creamy texture – has such a strong smell that it is very rarely served in restaurants. Instead durians are bought from street vendors or in fresh markets, then eaten outdoors or at home.

International cuisines

Almost any world cuisine you can name can be found somewhere in Bangkok, including Chinese, Mexican, British, Cajun-Creole, Japanese, Korean, French, Italian, Indian, Spanish, German, Arabic and Swedish. Italian cooking is particularly well represented, with some restaurants even specialising in Tuscan, Sardinian and other regional styles. The city has some stellar modern European restaurants as well.

Although it originally hails from Japan, *sukiyaki* has taken on many Thai characteristics in Bangkok, where it's extremely popular. *Sukee* (as it's called in Thai) is found in restaurants where booths or round tables are centred around a large pot sitting on a gas burner. The pot is filled with a broth at the beginning of the meal and, once it's boiling, diners sitting

Durians

Dubbed the king of fruits by the Thais, yet avoided by many foreigners, the durian (*thurian* in Thai) belongs to the *Bombacaceae* family and is native only to Southeast Asia. The heavy, spiked shell holds five sections of kidney-shaped, yellow-coloured flesh. One of the most well-known descriptions of the fruit is by 19th-century British scientist Alfred Russell Wallace:

'Custard flavoured with almonds, intermingled with wafts of flavour that call to mind cream cheese, onion sauce, brown sherry and other incongruities… neither acid, nor sweet, nor juicy, yet one feels the want of none of these qualities for it is perfect as it is.'

Due to its strong odour, most Bangkok hotels, as well as all domestic and international airlines, prohibit the fruit from their premises.

around the pot begin adding raw ingredients – *wun sen* (cellophane noodles), egg, water spinach, cabbage, thinly sliced beef and seafood – to the hot broth using chopsticks. When cooked, the diners then dip them into a Japanese-influenced sesame-chilli-garlic sauce.

WHAT TO DRINK

Non-alcoholic beverages

All restaurants serve purified water, whether by the glass or by the bottle. Thai restaurants also offer a variety of juices and fruit shakes made from Thailand's abundant fresh fruits, including most commonly mandarin orange, watermelon, pineapple, guava, papaya, mango, sugar cane and, best of all, fresh coconut water served straight from the coconut.

Alcoholic drinks

Thai-owned breweries produce a number of locally sold beers, including both domestic brands and licensed international brands. Singha, the country's oldest and most well-known label, packs a punch at 6 percent alcohol, outdone only by less expensive Chang (7 percent). Dutch giant Heineken, which co-operates a brewery just outside Bangkok, ranks third in sales after Singha and Chang. Various imported beers, including Mexico's Corona, German, British and US craft, can be found in the city's more upmarket bars and restaurants. Beer Lao, from Laos, is a tasty pick in cheaper bars. Draught beer (*bia sot*, literally 'fresh beer') is available in many Bangkok pubs and restaurants.

Sangsom, a popular and inexpensive 'whisky' (actually made with sugar cane, so technically a rum) made in Thailand, has an alcoholic content of 35 percent and is popular with working-class Thais and university students. Spey Royal and 100

Pipers cost a bit more and are distilled to resemble the taste of malt whisky. Thai whiskies are almost always ordered by the bottle. Some restaurants offer a special price for ordering a set that includes a bottle of whisky, ice and mixers.

Imported wines, notably from France, Italy, the US, Australia and Chile, are commonly available in wine shops and many restaurants. The government, however, levy a huge tax, and, while the choice available is impressive, the price of wine is probably the biggest downside of Bangkok dining.

Sticky rice and mango is a Thai classic

TO HELP YOU ORDER...

Do you have …? **Mee … mai?**
I eat only vegetarian food. **Chan kin jeh.**
Not spicy. **Mai phet.**
The bill, please. **Kep taang duay.**
I'd like a/an/some … **Khaw …**

beer **bia**	iced coffee **kaa-fae yen**
cup **thuay**	iced tea **chaa yen**
fork **sawm**	fruit **phon-la-mai**
glass **kaew**	menu **meh-noo**
hot coffee **kaa-fae rawn**	spoon **chawn**
hot tea **chaa rawn**	steamed rice **khao suay**
ice **naam khaen**	water **naam**

...AND READ THE MENU

kaeng khiaw-waan kai green curry with chicken

kaeng phet kai/neua red curry with chicken/beef

kai phat bai ka-phrao chicken stir-fried with hot chillies

kai phat khing chicken stir-fried with ginger and mild chillies

kai phat met ma-muang himaphaan chicken stir-fried with dried chillies and cashews

kai thawt fried chicken

kai yaang grilled chicken

khai dao fried egg

khai jiaw Thai-style omelette

khao phat kai/moo fried rice with chicken/pork

khao tom moo/kung rice soup with pork/prawns

kluay thawt batter-fried bananas

kuaytiaw phat see-yu stir-fried rice noodles

kung phao grilled prawns

moo krawp crisp-fried pork

moo yang grilled pork

naam kluay pan banana shake

naam taeng-moh pan watermelon shake

phat phak stir-fried vegetables

phat phak buay leng stir-fried Chinese spinach

phat phak bung fai daeng water spinach stir-fried with chillies, garlic and soy sauce

phat thai rice noodles stir-fried with tofu, bean sprouts, egg, dried shrimp

phrik naam plaa chillies in fish sauce

som-tam spicy green papaya salad

tom kha kai galangal and coconut soup with chicken

tom yam khung spicy lemongrass soup with prawns

yam plaa duk foo spicy catfish salad

PLACES TO EAT

Price ranges given below are based on a three-course meal for one, without drinks (alcoholic beverages can raise the bill significantly) or tips.

$$$$ over US$50	**$$$** US$20–50
$$ US$10–20	**$** below US$10

KO RATTANAKOSIN

The Deck $$$ *Arun Residence, 36–38 Soi Pratoo Nok Yoong, Maharat Road; tel: 0-2221 9158; www.arunresidence.com.* In a great river location, near Wat Pho, this restaurant is one of the best places to watch the sun set behind Wat Arun. It has a small but delicious menu of Thai specials. There are good views, too, from the rooftop bar.

Krisa $ *Na Phra Lan Road; tel: 0-2225 2680.* This tiny café has a perfect position opposite the Grand Palace to offer some aircondiitioned respite from the heat. They serve decent Thai standards like green curry and phat Thai, along with fruit juices and beers. Despite its tourist-friendly location, it's busy with local workers, which helps keep prices down.

CHINATOWN AND AROUND

Hua Seng Hong Yaowaraj $$ *438 Charoen Krung Soi 14; tel: 0-2627 5030.* This raucous restaurant has marble-top tables, all-day dim sum and all manner of Chinese dishes, such as congee, hot-and-sour soup, barbecued pork, fish maw and braised-goose dishes. It's just down from Wat Mangkon Kamalawat.

Soi Texas Seafood $$ *Soi Padung Dao; daily 6pm–2am.* This Chinatown soi gets its name from the Texas Suki restaurant 50m/yds in, but is famous for two very busy stalls at its mouth. Sit amid the nighttime ambiance at Rut and Lek or T & K and enjoy excellent dishes such as curried crab and variations of seafood including charcoal-grilled and fried with garlic and chilli.

Thai Heng $ *50 metres/yds into Yaowarat Soi 8, opposite Wat Bamphen Chin Phrot; tel: 0-2222 6791.* This simple 80-year-old café has a big reputation for southern Chinese dishes such as Hainan chicken rice served with spicy nam jim dip and rice soaked in chicken fat, and Hainan sukiyaki of meat and veg in a peppery broth. Both are delicious.

THONBURI

Pa Sidaa $ *112/5 Trok Wang Lang; tel: 0-2412 7189; daily 9am–7pm (closed every other Sun).* Located in a market alley close to the pier, this small café is famous for its 11 versions of somtam, the fiery sour salad of green papaya laced with lime juice and chilli. It also has grilled meats and Thai salads.

Yok Yor Marina $$ *Soi Somdet Chao Phraya Soi 17, Thonburi, tel: 0-2863 0565, www.yokyor.co.th.* Opposite the River City shopping centre, this huge open-air complex hugs the riverbank. The atmosphere makes up for the uneven food quality, but some dishes like *haw mok* (fish steamed in banana leaves with curry paste) stand out. They have live music, and patrons can choose to board the nightly 8pm dinner cruise boat for a small surcharge.

OLD BANGKOK AND DUSIT

Chon $$$ *The Siam hotel, 3/2 Thanon Khao; tel: 0-2206 6999; www.thesiamhotel.com; daily noon–11pm.* In a beautifully preserved traditional wooden house with antique decor, his riverside restaurant serves well prepared Thai classics. Pomelo salad and crab red curry are both good choices. The hotel shuttle boat runs from Saphan Taksin, and can be booked to stop at other piers.

Chote Chitr $$ *146 Phraeng Phuton Road, tel: 0-2221 4082.* Classic Thai cuisine is the forte here. Recipes that are slowly disappearing elsewhere in Bangkok, such as *mee krawp* (crisp-fried rice noodles in coconut sauce) and *yam hua phlee* (banana-flower salad), are well preserved.

Kaolang Home Kitchen $$ *2 Si Ayuthaya Road, Thewet, tel: 0-2281 9228.* On a rambling wooden deck overlooking the river, Kaolang specialises in fresh seafood. The atmosphere is totally relaxed for a long, leisurely meal of *tom yam* (prawn and lemongrass soup), *phat phak bung fai daeng* (water spinach flash-fried in bean sauce, garlic and chillies) and cold beer. It's located behind the National Library at the end of Si Ayutthaya Road.

Pen Thai Food $ *229 Soi Rambuttri; tel: 0-2282 2320.* Khun Siti-chai displays his food in metal pots and trays outside his shop-house on a street parallel to Khao San Road. Sit at one of the few tables and tuck into specialities like spicy catfish curry, soups and deep-fried fish, starting from B30 per dish.

Roti-Mataba $ *Phra Arthit Road.* Opposite Santichaiprakan Park, this narrow two-storey restaurant serves excellent southern Thai-style curries with *roti*, an Indian-influenced flatbread wrap. Rice dishes are also available. The upstairs dining room is air-conditioned, the downstairs is alfresco.

Thip Samai Phat Thai $ *313 Mahachai Road, tel: 0-2221 6280; daily 5.30pm–3.30am.* This humble street-side vendor near Ma-hakan Fort has been serving Bangkok's most famous *phat thai* (literally 'Thai-fried' – slender rice noodles stir-fried with tofu, bean sprouts, peanuts and prawns) for over 40 years. Choose among seven kinds, including the house version, combining fresh prawns, fresh crab, prawn roe, squid and sliced green mango. Try the delicious freshly squeezed orange juice or frozen coconut juice.

CENTRAL BANGKOK

Le Beaulieu $$$$ *Athénée Office Tower, 63 Wireless Road; tel: 08-1362 1362; www.le-beaulieu.com.* Hervé Frerard is perhaps the best French chef in the city, and he has a cosy, minimalist restaurant to show off skillful plates like roasted Anjou pigeon with truffle sauce. Outside there's a long bar with snackier items and chill out sounds.

Gaggan $$$$ *68/1 Soi Langsuan; tel: 0-2652 1700; www.eatat-gaggan.com.* These spectacular 'progressive Indian' creations by the El Bulli-inspired Gaggan Anand are among the world's finest dishes to emerge from the sub-continent. His tikka masala, cooked sous vide, with makani foam is stunning, coming as part of a set menu with other dishes like roasted foie gras with raspberry chutney. The setting is cool, too, in a summer-house interior of white woods and rattan. There's a small roof terrace for pre- or post-dinner drinks.

Gianni's Ristorante $$$ *34/1 Soi Tonson, off Ploenchit Road, tel: 0-2252 1619.* This extremely popular Italian restaurant just south of Chidlom Skytrain station needs advance reservations. The menu provides well-cooked Italian favourites like veal in tuna sauce, osso bucco, and tiramisu, and there's a good selection of wine.

La Monita Taqueria $$ *888/26 Mahatun Plaza, Thanon Ploenchit; tel: 0-2650 9581; www.lamonita.com.* This small Mexican diner has bright blue and orange decor, and good burritos, nachos, wings and Mexi or Cali tacos. The friendly atmosphere is helped along with with mojitos and beer. They also own the equally vibrant Spanish restaurant El Osito next door.

Soi Polo Fried Chicken $ *137/1–3 Soi Polo, Withayu Road, tel: 0-1252 2252.* A legend among local office workers, in addition to their signature garlic-heaped fried chicken (possibly Bangkok's best), Polo prepares delicious *somtam* (spicy green papaya salad), *laap* (sautéed minced chicken or duck in savoury herbs and spices) and other Isan standards.

Sra Bua $$$$ *Siam Kempinski Hotel, 991/9 Rama I Road; tel: 0-2162 9000; www.kempinskibangkok.com.* There's a theatrical and very tasty approach to local cuisine at this outlet of Copenhagen's Michelin-starred Thai restaurant, Kiin Kiin. Plates like green curry mousse, tom klong soup served as jellies, and red curry ice cream are playfully available as set menus with or without wine pairings.

Zuma $$$$ *St Regis Hotel, 159 Thanon Ratchadamri; tel: 0-2252 4707; www.zumarestaurant.com.* It's all natural woods and granite at this branch of London's modern Japanese. Top quality product includes miso marinated black cod to eat with hot, cold and sparkling sakes. There's an electro soundtrack and a bar that extends through full wall windows to a split level garden with sofas and ornamental trees.

SILOM AND BANGRAK

Aoi $$$ *132/10–11 Silom Soi 6; tel: 0-2235 2321; www.aoi-bkk. com.* Black stone walkways lead to a downstairs sushi bar and two floors of private and semi-private rooms above. All serve excellent Japanese food, including popular set meals. There are several other branches around town.

Eat Me $$$ *Soi Phiphat 2, off Convent Road, Silom, tel: 0-2238 0931,* www.eatmerestaurant.com. Chic and elegant Australian-owned restaurant serving a fusion menu that makes a welcome change from spicy Thai food. The dishes are tasty, inventive and beautifully served. It's always busy, so book ahead.

Harmonique $$ *34 Soi 24, Charoen Krung Road, tel: 0-2237 8175.* A round-doored former Chinese residence near the main post office is the setting for this cosy getaway from busy Charoen Krung Road. Well-prepared Thai and Chinese dishes are served at Hokkien-style marble-topped tables.

Issaya Siamese Club $$$$ *4 Soi Sri Aksorn, Chua Ploeng Road;* 0-2672 9040; www.issaya.com. Ian Kittichai, Thailand's best known home-grown chef, opened his signature Bangkok outlet following successes in Europe and the US. The beautiful 100 year-old wooden house setting is perfect for enjoying modern Thai interpretations including red chilli-glazed baby back ribs infused with *tom yum* broth.

Khrua Aroy Aroy $ *Pan Road, off Silom Road, tel: 0-2635 2365.* This traditional Thai eatery opposite Wat Maha Uma Devi displays the day's curries and soups in a row of large pots. Of particular note is the *khanom jeen yaa* (thin rice noodles ladled with fish curry) and *thawt man plaa* (fried fishcakes with peanut-cucumber sauce). Lunchtime is the best time to visit, though it's open until 9pm.

Nahm $$$$ *Metropolitan Hotel, 27 Thanon Sathorn Tai; tel: 0-2625 3333;* www.comohotels.com/metropolitanbangkok. Run by Australian chef David Thompson, this is a branch of what was Europe's first Michelin-starred Thai restaurant. The brilliant traditional menu features regional specialities, with flavours such as northern pork, prawn and tamarind relish served with braised mackerel, sweet pork, crispy acacia and soft boiled eggs. Sit inside or by the outdoor pool.

Sirocco $$$$ *63/F, Lebua at State Tower, 1055/111 Silom Road; tel: 0-2624 9555;* www.thedomebkk.com. The breathtaking views from this 200m (656ft) high rooftop restaurant provide a world class setting for Mediterranean food. Also in the complex are the classy Distil Bar, which has good seafood; Breeze for modern Asian; and very accomplished modern European at Mezzaluna.

SUKHUMVIT ROAD

Bo.lan $$$$ *42 Soi Pichai Ronnarong, Sukhumvit Soi 26; tel: 0-2260 2962;* www.bo.lan.com. This cute old house restaurant is run by chefs once of London's Michelin-starred Thai restaurant Nahm. The choice of set or a la carte menu starts with a traditional herb liquor and continues through skillful regional dishes like sweet cured pork in coconut cream and deep-fried fish with an eye-watering spicy-sour dipping sauce.

New York Steakhouse $$$$ *JW Marriott, 4 Sukhumvit Soi 2; tel: 0-2656 7700;* www.marriott.com. Formal trappings of club-like dark woods and high-backed leather chairs set the scene for high quality, grain-fed Angus beef sliced tableside from a silver trolley. There's a long Martini list, fine wines and atmospheric black-and-white photos of the Big Apple on the walls. Booking is essential.

Opposite Mess Hall $$ *27/1 Sukhumvit Soi 51; tel: 0-2662 6330;* www.oppositebangkok.com. Popular chef Jess Barnes features down-to-earth dishes like smoked bone marrow dumplings with beef broth, pumpkin and fermented daikon, and steamed Chinese bun with fried tempeh, kimchi, sriracha mayo and scamorza cheese. Across the soi is its sister operation, the art bar WTF. Opposite Mess Hall is excellent, but tiny, and they don't take reservations, so there's a chance of waiting for a seat.

Ruen Mallika $$ *189 Sukhumvit Soi 22; tel: 0-2663 3211-2; www.ruen-mallika.com.* Rama I period wooden house with garden tables and traditional floor-cushion seating inside. Options include *kaeng tai pla* (pungent southern-style fish-stomach curry), which tastes better than it sounds, *mee krob* (sweet and herby crispy noodles) and deep-fried flowers.

Soi 38 Food Stalls $ *Sukhumvit Soi 38; daily 4pm–2am.* Handily placed beside the Thonglor Skytrain station, these rough-and-tumble food stalls provide one of Bangkok's best loved food hangouts. The options run from rice gruel, through spring rolls, crab salad and crispy pork, to nam kaeng sai (desserts with ice). It's a favourite haunt of people going to or leaving the bars of Thonglor, opposite.

Vientiane Kitchen $ *8 Soi 36, Sukhumvit Road, tel: 0-2258 6171.* A casual and popular restaurant offering fiery Lao-Isan favourites such as *kai yaang* (spicy grilled chicken), *laap* (spicy minced-meat salad) and *som-tam* (green papaya salad). The Lao-Isan garden-style setting is supplemented by a live band playing *maw lam* (traditional Lao-Isan folk music).

Water Library @ Grass $$$$ *Grass Thonglor, 264/1 Sukhumvit Soi 55 (Thonglor 12); tel: 0-2714 9292; www.mywaterlibrary.com.* The impressive flagship of a growing chain across the region, this place serves a sublime 12 course set menu using modern techniques and funky presentation to just 10 diners a night at a sushi style counter. The chefs perform in front of your eyes, as if on a small stage, delivering items such as Belon oysters with beurre blanc ice-cream, caviar and yuzu. Booking is essential.

A–Z TRAVEL TIPS

A Summary of Practical Information

A

ACCOMMODATION (see also Hotels on page 135)

Bangkok accommodation runs the gamut from backpacker guesthouses to world-class luxury hotels. At all price ranges, the city typically offers some of the best value anywhere in Asia. It's best to book in advance for the holiday periods at Christmas, New Year and Chinese New Year (Jan/Feb), and for the Songkran festival in mid-April. but rates are very elastic, so it is advisable to shop around, and in low season (May–Sept) discounts can be around 50 percent. Serviced apartments are also plentiful.

Major four- and five-star hotels hotels are commonly located around the Silom Road financial district, Siam Square, Sukhumvit Road, all of which are convenient for BTS Skytrain passengers, and along the Chao Phraya River. But these areas also have their share of mid-range and budget accommodation.

More extensive cheaper accommodation tends to be concentrated in Banglamphu close to Khao San Road, but here there is an increasing choice of more upmarket options, most of which have a boutique feel, thanks to planning restrictions. Some predict the accommodation profile in this area and in Chinatown may alter with the extension of the mass transit underground system, which is due to begin operating by 2016.

---

single room **hawng diaw**
double room **hawng khoo**
I'd like a single/double room **Tawng-kaan hawng diaw/khoo**
with bathroom. **hawng naam nai tua.**
What's the rate per night? **Khaa hawng thao rai?**

AIRPORTS

Bangkok has two airports. Approximately 30km (19 miles) east of the city, **Suvarnabhumi Airport** (BKK; call centre tel: 0 2132 1888, departures tel: 0 2132 9324, arrivals tel: 0 2132 9328, help desk tel: 0 2132 3888; www.suvarnabhumiairport.com), is also known as New Bangkok International Airport (NBIA). The name is pronounced Suwannapoom. The airport handles most international flights, with several airlines flying from around the world. International departure taxes are included in tickets.

Road travel from the airport to most parts of Bangkok averages 30–45 minutes. Official airport taxis are air-conditioned and metered and operate round the clock. Ignore the touts and head for the official taxi booth outside on the first floor concourse. Join the queue and tell the person at the desk where you want to go to. A receipt will be issued, with the licence-plate number of the taxi and your destination in Thai written on it. Make sure the driver turns on the meter. At the end of your trip, pay what is on the meter plus the B50 airport surcharge and the highway toll fees (about B90 in total to downtown). Depending on traffic, an average fare from the airport to the city centre is around B450 (including toll fees and airport surcharge).

The Suvarnabhumi Airport Rail Link connects to the city at Phaya Thai station, where it links with the Skytrain system. There are two services: the Express Line (B90-150) and the City Line (B15-45), which calls at eight stations en route – Lat Krabang, Ban Thap Chang, Hua Mak, Ramkhamhaeng, Asoke, Makkasan, Ratchaprarop and Phaya Thai. It takes 30 minutes for the full journey. There are also BMTA public buses.

Some low budget carriers use **Don Mueang Airport** (DMK; tel: 0 2535 1111; www.donmueangairportthai.com) for both domestic and international flights, including Air Asia (www.airasia.com/th/en), Orient Thai (www.flyorientthai.com) and Nok Air (www.nok air.com).

For transport into the city (23km/14 miles) from Don Muang, passengers can choose to go by taxi (B200–350), railway (schedule varies; B12–39) or public bus (5am–11pm; B12).

Road transport between the two airports takes around 45 minutes. Taxi fare runs around B380, bus fare B35. Travel times can more than double during rush hours or during heavy rain, so be sure to leave plenty of time.

> I need a taxi. **Tawng-kaan rot taek-see.**
> How much is it to… ? **Pai… thao rai?**
> Does this bus go to…? **Rot meh nee pai… mai?**

B

BARGAINING

Prices for goods for sale at markets and street stalls are usually negotiable and bargaining is expected. A genuine smile will go a long way towards obtaining a good price.

> I want this one. **Khaw an-nee.**
> Can I look at that one? **Khaw doo an-nan?**
> small/too small **lek/lek pai**
> large/too large **yai/yai pai**
> Let me see another colour please. **Khaw doo see eun?**
> Can you lower the price? **Lot raakhaa dai mai?**
> expensive/too expensive **phaeng/phaeng pai**
> cheap **thook**

BUDGETING FOR YOUR TRIP

Bangkok's prices are rising rapidly, but you can still find bargains. The following is meant only as a rough guide. There are approximately THB55 to £1 sterling and THB32 to the US dollar.

Accommodation. Room rates at the average mid-range hotel in popular areas run to approximately THB2,000–3,000 a night.

Some hotels add a 10 percent service charge and 7 percent hotel tax (one of the lowest in the region).

Meals and drinks. Breakfast or lunch in a local Thai restaurant runs to no more than THB100 per person, dinner about THB200. A multi-course meal in a mid-range Thai restaurant for tourists costs around THB400 per person, not including alcoholic beverages. Compared to food, alcoholic drinks are pricey in Bangkok: THB60–120 for a 750ml bottle of beer. Owing to the fact that they are heavily taxed, imported liquors and wine are likely to cost much more in Bangkok than in your home country.

Entertainment. Typical museum entry fees are THB40–100. Entry to many Buddhist temples is free, with Wat Pho (THB100), Wat Arun (THB50) and Wat Phra Kaew (THB500) the most notable exceptions. Cinema tickets cost from THB150, and dance clubs with cover charges cost from THB300 (including one or two drinks).

Transport. Most metered taxi rides around the city cost under THB150, or to one of the airports THB200–300. Three-wheeled motorcycle taxis called *tuk-tuks* charge about the same as metered taxis, but you must bargain the fare first. Two-wheeled motorcycle taxis in smaller streets charge THB10–20 per ride. City buses charge from around THB8–10 for non-air-conditioned routes, otherwise THB12–22. The BTS Skytrain costs THB16–40 depending on distance, while the newer MRTA (Metro) subway is THB16–45.

C

CAR HIRE (RENTAL)

You need an international licence to drive in Thailand, and Bangkok can be challenging if you are not used to city driving. Count on THB800 per day for a small car (check that insurance is included). A driver costs an extra THB300–500 per day.

Recommended car-hire companies include:

Avis tel: 0-2255 5300; www.avisthailand.com

Sathorn Car Rent tel: 0-2633 8888

CLIMATE

Bangkok sits on a flat, humid river delta, with tropical temperatures all year round. The southwest monsoon typically sweeps in from the Indian Ocean in May and lasts until mid- to late October. During this season the heaviest rainfall usually occurs during August and September. Beginning in December, rains from a second monsoon from the northeast bypass Bangkok but bring lower relative temperatures until mid-February. With both monsoons gone, much higher relative temperatures follow from March to May before the whole cycle begins again. The following chart shows the average number of rainy days each month:

	J	F	M	A	M	J	J	A	S	O	N	D
Rainy days	2	2	4	5	14	16	19	21	23	17	7	1

CLOTHING

Casual dress is acceptable for almost all occasions in Bangkok. Because of the hot, humid climate, lightweight, breathable fabrics are the most comfortable option. Upmarket restaurants and clubs frown on shorts or sandals. Shorts (men and women) and plunging necklines are considered culturally unacceptable for Buddhist temple visits. Shoes must be removed before entering Buddhist shrine halls or private homes.

CRIME AND SAFETY (see also Emergencies)

Crime against tourists is relatively rare in Bangkok. None of the city's districts need to be considered 'off limits' for security reasons. Guard your belongings against pickpockets on crowded buses or in markets, and in the Khao San Road area. Avoid any stranger who brings up the topic of gems or tailor shops, as these are virtually always an introduction to a scam.

Call the police! **Khaw jaeng tam-ruat!**
Help! **Chuay duay!**
Call a doctor! **Khaw riak maw!**
Danger! **Antaraai!**

D

DISABLED TRAVELLERS

There are signs of slow improvement in Bangkok's facilities for disabled people, such as more modified toilets, buildings with wheelchair ramps and lifts in metro stations (although few on the Skytrain network). However, Bangkok's uneven pavements are full of obstructions, which makes getting around difficult, and it may be preferable to travel with a companion. Online resources such as www.accessiblethailand. com are useful for such things as hotels and local carers or assistants.

E

ELECTRICITY

Thailand's power supply is 220V, 50 cycles. Most wall outlets take dual-pin plugs, both round and flat. Adaptors and voltage converters are available at most hotels or they can be purchased at local shops selling electrical supplies. A majority of hotels have an electrical outlet for shavers; some have 110V sockets, too.

EMBASSIES AND CONSULATES

Be sure to phone before visiting, as most embassies are open to the public only in the morning or afternoon.

Australia: 37 Sathon Tai Road, tel: 0-2344 6300; www.thailand.
embassy.gov.au.
Canada: 15th floor, Abdulrahim Building, 990 Rama IV Road, tel:
0-2646 4300; www.canadainternational.gc.ca/thailand-thailande.
South Africa: 12 A Floor, M-Thai Tower, All Seasons Place, 87 Withayu (Wireless) Road, tel: 0-2659 2900; www.dirco.gov.za.
UK: 14 Withayu (Wireless) Road, tel: 0-2305 8333; www.ukba.home
office.gov.uk (visas).
US: 120–122 Withayu (Wireless) Road, tel: 0-2205 4000, http://bang
kok.usembassy.gov.

EMERGENCIES (see also Crime and safety)

Emergency numbers in Bangkok:
Police (and Ambulance) **191**; Tourist Police **1155**; Fire **195**.

G

GAY AND LESBIAN TRAVELLERS

Homosexuality is accepted by most Thais, particularly in Bangkok,
and there are no laws forbidding same-sex alliances. The city has the
most celebrated gay and lesbian scene in Asia. There are many bars
catering for gay men and a smaller number for lesbians. Utopia's
website (www.utopia-asia.com) is an excellent source of information
for gay and lesbian venues and events in Bangkok.

GETTING THERE (see also Airports)

By air. Suvarnabhumi Airport receives hundreds of international flights
daily from cities in Asia, Australia, Europe and the US. The national car-
rier, Thai Airways International (THAI; tel: 0-2288 7000; www.thaiair.
com), has the most extensive route network and flight schedule. Some
low budget carriers, including Air Asia (www.airasia.com/th/en), use
Don Mueang Airport for international flights, particularly around the
region, but also increasingly for destinations further afield.

By rail. The State Railway of Thailand (tel: 0-2222 0175, hotline: 1690; www.railway.co.th) operates cheap and reliable trains. There are daily trains from Malaysia to Bangkok's Hualamphong Station.

GUIDES AND TOURS

Day tours. Most hotels and guesthouses can arrange day tours by car or van. Less expensive tours are pre-arranged, while customised tours cost only a little more. The larger hotels have their own tour desks with detailed tour itineraries and staff who can help you select the most appropriate one. Visitors can also contact outside tour operators such as World Travel Service (1053 Charoen Krung Road; tel: 0-2233 5900; www.worldtravelservice.co.th), which was founded in 1947 and is one of Bangkok's largest agencies.

River and Canal Tours. Boat tours of the Chao Phraya River and the linking canals of Khlong Bangkok Yai, Khlong Bangkok Noi and Khlong Om are a popular way of seeing parts of the city that aren't easily visited by road. Longtail boats moored at Tha Chang, Tha Tien and Tha Banglamphu river piers offer standard and customised river/canal tours for around THB700–800 per hour.

Bicycle Tours. Co Van Kessel (tel: 0-2639 7351; www.covankessel. com) offers daily bike trips around Bangkok, including Chinatown and Thonburi's canalside districts and gardens.

We'd like an English-speaking guide/an English interpreter
Rao yaak dai phoo nam thiaw/laam thee phootphaasaa thai dai.

H

HEALTH AND MEDICAL CARE

Thailand requires no vaccinations prior to arrival. Health professionals recommend vaccinations for hepatitis A and B if you plan to stay in Thailand more than a month. Consult the World Health Organisation (www.who.int/en) for any current health warnings for Thailand. Aside from having Thailand's best health-care facilities, Bangkok is a well-known destination for medical tourism.

Hospitals. US-accredited **Bumrungrad International** (33 Soi 3, Sukhumvit Road; tel: 0-2667 1000; www.bumrungrad.com) is the most luxurious hospital complex in the city. Other recommended hospitals include **Mission Hospital** (430 Phitsanulok Road; tel: 0-2282 1100; www.mission-hospital.org), **Samitivej Sukhumvit Hospital** (133 Soi 49, Sukhumvit Road; tel: 0-2711 8181; www.sami tivejhospitals.com) and **Bangkok Hospital** (2 Soi 47, New Phetburi Road; tel: 0-2310 3000; www.bangkokhospital.com). They all offer 24-hour emergency services along with dental and ophthalmologi-cal treatment facilities.

Pharmacies. Open 24 hours in hospitals and Foodland Supermar-ket Pharmacy (1413 Soi 5, Sukhumvit Road; tel: 0-2254 2247).

---

pharmacy **raan khaai yaa**
hospital **rohng phayaabaan**
doctor **maw**
Where's the nearest pharmacy? **Raan khaai yaa klai-sut yoo thee nai?**
I need a doctor/dentist. **Chan tawng-kaan maw/ maw fan.**
an ambulance **rot phayaabaan**
an upset stomach **thawng sia**
a fever **pen khai**

L

LANGUAGE

English is widely used in hotels and shops, but it is always greatly appreciated when visitors try to speak some Thai. Bangkokians speak the Central Thai dialect, one of four major Thai dialects in Thailand. Thai has its own script with 44 consonants and 32 vowels. It's also a tonal language, so the meaning of a word or syllable may be altered by speaking that word with one of five different tones. Thai has five tones: low tone, level or mid tone, falling tone, high tone and rising tone. Depending on the tone, for example, the word *mai* might mean 'new', 'burn', 'wood' or 'not'.

To be polite, men should end each sentence with the politening syllable *khrap*. Women should end each sentence with *kha*.

M

MAPS

Free maps are available at hotel reception counters. Detailed city maps may be purchased at bookshops throughout Bangkok. The most useful maps will have entries labelled in both English and Thai.

MEDIA

Newspapers. Two English-language dailies are widely available, *Bangkok Post* and *The Nation*. *The International New York Times* (Singapore edition) can be found in most hotel news-stands.

Listing magazines. Free English-language weekly *BK Magazine* (www.bkmagazine.com) and monthly *Bangkok 101* have good listings and reviews of sights, restaurants and happenings.

MONEY

Currency. The Thai baht (THB) is the national currency. Paper notes are colour-coded and come in denominations of THB20 (green), THB50 (blue), THB100 (red), THB500 (purple) and THB1,000 (brown). 1-, 2, 5- and 10-baht coins are also widely circulated, and the baht is further divided into 100 satang, available as 25-satang and

50-satang coins.

Banks. All Thai banks offer foreign exchange services at branches throughout the city. The most foreigner-friendly are Bank of Ayudhya, Bangkok Bank, KasikornBank and Siam Commercial Bank. Most banks are open Mon–Fri 8.30am–3.30pm, but some branches maintain exchange booths open until 8pm.

Cash dispensers (ATMs). Facilities for using your debit or credit card to withdraw cash automatically function 24 hours a day throughout the city. Most will accept international cards and as such are the most convenient way for foreign visitors to withdraw cash as needed. The exchange rate for cash dispensers is better than the rate at exchange booths, and transaction fees are low.

Credit cards. Visa and MasterCard credit cards are accepted at most hotels and department stores, luxury restaurants and upmarket shops. American Express is less widely accepted.

Currency exchange. Cash dispensers are the most convenient and least costly way to obtain cash in Bangkok, but visitors may also change major foreign currencies (cash or travellers' cheques) at local banks or at bank-owned foreign-exchange booths at the airports and in areas where there are many tourists (such as Sukhumvit, Silom and Khao San roads). Banks and exchange booths charge a commission for cashing travellers' cheques.

Can I pay with this credit card? **Jaai pen bat credit yang nee dai mai?**

I want to change some pounds/dollars **Yaak ja laek plian pound/dollar.**

Where's the nearest bank? **Thanaakhaan klai-sut yoo thee nai?**

Is there a cash machine near here? **Mee khreuang atm klai thee nee mai?**

How much is that? **Nee raakhaa thao rai?**

O

OPENING TIMES

Banks. Monday–Friday 8.30am–3.30pm. Foreign-exchange booths may stay open until 8pm.

Shops. Most shops are open Monday–Saturday 10am–6pm. Department stores may be open as late as 10pm.

Offices. Government and business offices generally open Monday–Friday 8.30am–4.30pm. Some also open Saturday 8.30am–noon. Most government offices take an unofficial lunch break noon–1pm.

Nightspots. Bars are permitted to stay open until midnight, live music clubs until 1am and discos/dance clubs until 2am.

P

POLICE (see also Emergencies and Crime and safety)

The Royal Thai Police wear brown uniforms. They can be reached via a three-digit hotline number, 191. Most members of the police speak very little English.

It is best to report thefts or other criminal complaints to the Tourist Police, a separate, English-speaking force trained to deal with foreigners. The Tourist Police can be reached by dialling 1155 any time of day or night.

police **tam-ruat**
Tourist Police **tam-ruat thawng thiaw**
Where's the nearest police station? **Sathaanee tam-ruat thee klai-sut yoo thee nai?**
I've lost my... **...haai**
wallet/bag/passport. **kra-bao ngoen/ kra-bao/nang seu doen thaang.**

POST OFFICES

Bangkok's main post office on Charoen Krung Road is open Monday–Friday 8am–8pm, weekends and holidays 8am–1pm. Branch post offices, open weekdays only, can be found around the city. Almost all the big hotels offer postal services, and newsagents sell stamps.

Thailand's domestic and international postal services are fast, efficient and inexpensive. Most post offices also offer packaging materials and packing services, as well as poste restante mail.

PUBLIC HOLIDAYS

Banks and government offices, along with some businesses, are closed on the following public holidays (many are fixed to the lunar calendar so differ each year):

1 January New Year's Day
January/February Chinese New Year (first lunar month)
March Magha Puja (full moon of the third lunar month)
6 April Chakri Day
May Vesakha Puja (full moon of the sixth lunar month)
5 May Coronation Day
July Asalha Puja (full moon of the eighth lunar month)
Vassa (day after the full moon)
12 August Queen's Birthday
23 October Chulalongkorn Day
5 December King's Birthday
10 December Constitution Day

R

RELIGION

An estimated 90 percent of Bangkokians profess belief in Theravada Buddhism, the world's oldest and most traditional Buddhist sect. Theravada Buddhists believe that individuals work out their own paths to *nibbana* (nirvana) through a combination of good works, meditation and study of the *dhamma* or Buddhist philosophy. Buddhist monks live ascetic lives in more than 300 monasteries *(wat)* that are dotted around the city.

Around 4 percent of city residents are Muslims, mostly of Malay or Indian descent, and mosques are relatively common in some areas of Bangkok, particularly Bangrak. Many Chinese residents practise Mahayana Buddhism, and there is also a significant number of Sikhs living in the city, along with a sprinkling of Vietnamese and Cambodian Roman Catholics.

T

TELEPHONES

The privately owned, government-subsidised Telephone Organisation of Thailand (TOT) operates land-based telephone services in Thailand. Several GSM-based mobile phone services are available; the most popular are True and AIS. SIM cards may be purchased locally and used with any mobile phone that isn't SIM-locked. Mobile phones and SIM cards with prepaid, short-term accounts may be purchased inexpensively at any department store or mobile phone shop.

The country code for Thailand is 66. Add a 0 before the phone number to call landlines and 08 before mobile numbers. If dialling Bangkok from abroad, omit the 0 in both cases.

If dialling abroad from a Bangkok land line, you must dial the international access code 001 before the country code. If dialling from a mobile phone, the international access code is not necessary.

The relatively few phone kiosks that do accept coins nowadays accept 1-, 5- and 10-baht coins as standard. More common are phonecard kiosks, which accept cards that can be purchased at any convenience store in denominations ranging from THB40 to THB400.

Hotels usually add surcharges of up to 50 percent over the gazetted phone rates. The least expensive way to call internationally is to use internet phone services, available at most internet cafes.

TIME ZONES

Bangkok's time zone is GMT +7 all year. Times are often written using the 24-hour clock (for example, 8pm may be written 2000).

TIPPING

Tipping is never automatic, especially in upmarket hotels and restaurants, where a 10 percent service charge is usually added to the bill. Where there is no service charge, Bangkokians may leave some loose change (no more than THB100) when paying a large restaurant bill, and no more than THB20 in small cafés. Hotel staff and taxi drivers will appreciate a THB20 per bag tip for luggage assistance, although in neither case is it mandatory.

TOILETS

Most hotels, restaurants and public conveniences have regular sit-down toilets, but cheaper guesthouses, especially upcountry, may have the more traditional 'squat' toilet. Toilet stalls in most public conveniences are not equipped with toilet paper; you're expected to bring your own tissue or buy some from a vending machine or from staff sitting out front.

toilet (restroom) **hawng naam**
Where are the toilets? **Hawng naam yoo thee nai?**

TOURIST INFORMATION

The city government's **Bangkok Tourist Division** (BTD; 17/1 Phra Athit Road; open Mon–Fri 9am–7pm, Sat–Sun 9am–5pm; tel: 0-2225 7612; www.bangkoktourist.com) has a small office in Banglamphu stocked with free maps, brochures and other useful information on the city. The BTD also maintains counters in Suvarnabhumi Airport, opposite Wat Phra Kaew and at a few shopping centres around the city.

Orientated towards tourism both in Bangkok and the provinces, the **Tourist Authority of Thailand** (TAT; 1600 New Phetchaburi Road, Makkasan; tel: 0-2250 5500; www.tourismthailand.org) also distributes printed information on Bangkok's sights and culture. There is a second branch in Banghlamphu (Ratchadamnoen Nok Road; open daily 8.30am–4.30pm; tel: 0-2283 1555, ext 1556) adjacent to Ratchadamnoen Boxing Stadium, and information kiosks (open daily 8am–midnight) at Suvarnabhumi and Don Mueang airports. The TAT maintains a Tourist Assistance Centre daily 8am–8pm (tel: 1672), outside these hours contact the Tourist Police (tel: 1155).

TRANSPORT

Boat. Large longtail boats ply regular routes along a few of Bangkok's canals, much like a water-borne bus service, with fares from THB10–25. The most extensive services are along Khlong Saen Saep, which runs east–west across much of the city from Banglamphu to Bang Kapi, more or less parallel to Sukhumvit Road.

Along the Chao Phraya River, larger cruisers operated by Chao Phraya Express Boat (tel: 0-2445 8888; www.chaophrayaexpressboat.com; fares THB10–40) run approximately every 15 minutes, Mon-Fri 6am–8pm, Sat-Sun 6am-7pm. Cross-river ferries are available at many points along the river, costing THB4 per crossing.

Longtail boats can also be chartered along both river and canals for around THB500–800 per hour.

Bus. The Bangkok Mass Transit Authority (BMTA; tel: 1348; www.bmta.co.th) operates a large fleet of buses that run along more than 100 established routes all over the city. Fares are THB8–25 per trip depending on how far you're going and the type of bus. BMTA buses are relatively comfortable but slow. Most buses operate daily 5am–11pm but there are also a few all-night buses on certain routes. Bus maps showing the numbered routes are available for purchase at most bookshops in Bangkok.

Metro. The Metropolitan Rapid Transit Authority (MRTA; tel: 0-2716 4044; www.mrta.co.th) operates a subway system from Hualamphong Railway Station to Bang Seu Railway Station, with extensions and more lines under construction. Trains operate daily 6am–midnight and fares are THB16–41 depending on distance travelled. Four of the 18 stations connect with the Skytrain.

Skytrain. The BTS Skytrain (tel: 0-2617 6000; www.bts.co.th), an elevated railway with two intersecting lines, is a quick and efficient way to travel across the city. The Sukhumvit Line runs from Mo Chit, near Chatuchak Park in northern Bangkok, to Bearing in the east. The Silom Line starts at the National Stadium, near Siam Square, and continues across the Chao Phraya River to Bang Wa in Thonburi. The two lines intersect at Siam Station at Siam Square.

Trains run daily 6am–midnight and fares are THB15–42. A one-day pass (THB130) allows unlimited travel and there's a Rabbit Card to which you can add discounted multi-trip packages running from B405 for 15 trips to B1,100 for 50 trips.

Taxi. Metered taxis charge THB35 at flagfall for the first 2km (1.5 miles), then around THB5 per km. If traffic is moving slowly, a small per-minute surcharge kicks in. If the driver uses a tollway, the passenger pays the charges (THB30–75).

V

VISAS AND ENTRY REQUIREMENTS

All foreign visitors to Thailand must carry a passport valid for at least six months after their arrival. Citizens of many countries may visit Thailand without any visa for 15–90 days, depending on the country (permission to stay is granted on arrival). For visits longer than your allowance, you should obtain Thailand's 60-day Tourist Visa from a Thai consulate or embassy abroad. For a comprehensive look at visa types visit the Ministry of Foreign Affairs website (www.mfa.go.th).

The importation of illegal drugs, firearms and pornographic media is forbidden. Foreign currency over US$20,000 entering or leaving the country should be declared. Thai currency leaving the country is limited to B50,000. VAT refunds on items bought in Thailand are available on completion of necessary paperwork at the airport.

Buddha images, art and antiques acquired in Thailand require an export licence from the Department of Fine Arts (in the National Museum at 4 Na Phra That Road; tel: 0-2226 1661) before they are taken out of the country. Sometimes this can be arranged by the vendor. Antique Buddha images cannot be taken out at all. The licensing procedure takes three to five days.

WEBSITES AND INTERNET ACCESS

Internet centres with inexpensive rates (average THB30/hour) are plentiful throughout Bangkok. Many hotels also offer internet connections at much higher rates.

Wi-fi services are expanding rapidly in Bangkok and are widely available in the Khao San Road, Silom, Sukhhumvit and other central areas. Many coffee shops, including all branches of Starbucks and Coffee World, and increasing numbers of places to stay – even small hotels and guest houses – offer free wi-fi.

Recommended websites for more information on Bangkok include:

www.bangkokpost.com: Bangkok Post newspaper

www.bkmagazine.com: BK Magazine

www.thaivisa.com/forum: Thai Visa Expat Forum

www.tourismthailand.org: Tourism Authority of Thailand

YOUTH HOSTELS

Bangkok has several members of Hostelling International (www.hi hostels.com).

Recommended Hotels

Hotels are clustered in four main areas: along Silom, Surawong and Sathon roads, Sukhumvit Road between Soi 1 and Soi 33, near Siam Square and Pratunam, and on the banks of the Chao Phraya River. Hundreds of inexpensive guesthouses can be found in the city, along with a growing number of boutique properties, often in converted old buildings.

It's a good idea to stay near one of the Skytrain lines, and if you are staying in the Khao San area, to look for quieter rooms away from the party action.

Book well in advance for the December– April peak season, especially around Christmas. At other times, there are usually discounted rates. As usual, websites such as www.agoda.com and www.trivago.com are often cheaper than booking directly.

Larger hotels accept international credit cards, while many small hotels and guesthouses will insist on cash. A 10 percent service charge and 7 percent tax are typically added to the room bill as you go further up the range. Price guides below are for a standard double room without breakfast and taxes.

$$$$$	over US$240
$$$$	US$130–240
$$$	US$70–130
$$	US$35–70
$	below US$35

KO RATTAKOSIN

Arun Residence $$$ *36–38 Soi Pratoo Nok Yoong, Maharat Road; tel: 0-2221 9158; www.arunresidence.com.* Delightful boutique hotel a couple of minutes' walk from Wat Pho and the Grand Palace, commanding great views over the river towards Wat Arun. The pleasant and comfortable rooms, in a renovated Sino-Portugese mansion, are decorated in an elegant contemporary colonial style, and feature all modern amenities. The Deck restaurant (see page 109) has good food.

Chakrabongse Villas $$$$$ *396 Maharat Road; tel: 0-2225 1290;* www.chakrabongsevillas.com. Built in 1908, this compound of four Thai-style villas was once the home of a Thai prince (some of his family still live here). The elegant setting, with beautiful gardens and a secluded pool, overlooks the river and Wat Arun. The Grand Palace is a 15-minute walk away.

CHINATOWN AND AROUND

River View Guest House $ *768 Soi Phanurangsi, Songwat Road; tel: 0-2234 5429;* www.riverviewbkk.com. Wedged between the fancier Silom area and bustling Chinatown, this eight-storey guesthouse is only separated from the Chao Phraya River by a sprawling Chinese temple. Rooms are functional and clean. Views from the inexpensive rooftop restaurant are superb.

Shanghai Mansion $$$ *479–81 Yaowarat Road; tel: 0-2221 2121;* www.shanghaimansion.com. This classy boutique hotel has an extravagant classical Chinese-style interior with lots of vibrant red and gold. The rooms have four-poster beds, there's a jazz lounge, free internet access and a spa.

THONBURI

Ibrik Resort $$ *256 Soi Wat Rakang, Arun Amarin Road; tel: 0-2848 9220;* www.ibrikresort.com. A tidy, all-white wooden cottage with only three large rooms and its feet in the river, so that you feel as though you are staying on a riverboat.

Peninsula $$$$$ *333 Charoen Nakhon Road; tel: 0-2861 2888;* http://bangkok.peninsula.com. The Pen's modern decor features high-quality contemporary Thai art and extremely grand proportions, with massive windows overlooking the riverside terrace. Rooms and suites are spacious and well equipped and come with dazzling river views. There's a top quality spa, a helipad on the roof, and the Chinese restaurant Mei Jeang is one of the best in town. The hotel shuttle boats link to the Saphan Taksin BTS station and express boat stop.

OLD BANGKOK AND DUSIT

Buddy Lodge $$ *265 Khao San Road; tel: 0-2629 4477; www.buddy lodge.com.* The original of Khao San's 'boutique' accommodation contains comfortable rooms with white-painted wood-and-brass decor hinting at early 20th-century Bangkok. The hotel offers something for everyone in its ground-floor complex, including a coffee shop/bookshop and a tattoo and piercing parlour.

D&D Inn $ *68–70 Khao San Road; tel: 0-2629 0526; www.khaosanby. com.* The rooftop swimming pool makes this place stand out at this price, and there's a bar and an open pavilion for traditional massage. The rooms have bathroom, air-conditioning, TV, fridge and IDD phone. It is bang in the middle of the Khao San action so expect noise.

Hotel De'Moc $ *78 Prachatipatai Road; tel: 0-2282 2831; www.hotel democ.com.* Built in 1962 the De'Moc (named after the Democracy Monument a few streets away) is a reliable two-star hotel with plain but comfortable rooms, a swimming pool, a small spa and a restaurant serving Thai, Chinese and Western food.

Old Bangkok Inn $$$ *609 Phra Sumen Road; tel: 0-2629 1787; www. oldbangkokinn.com.* The 10 rooms and suites here have a traditional Thai character, each with a floral or herb theme, from lemongrass to jasmine, and teak furniture and fittings. Some have split level accommodation with sleeping areas in the loft. Satellite TV, DVD players, internet, and computers are common to all. A good spot for the Golden Mount and Old City attractions.

Phranakorn Nornlen $$ *46 Thewet Soi 1, Krung Kasem Road; tel: 0-2628 8188; www.phranakorn-nornlen.com.* Small but utterly charming award-winning hotel in a wooden house with a peaceful courtyard. The rooms are comfortable and quiet, there is plenty of communal space, including a library/living room and a rooftop garden where the staff grow their own organic vegetables.

Riva Surya Bangkok $$$ *23 Phra Arthit Road; tel: 0-2633 5000; www.rivasuryabangkok.com.* Riva's riverside spot is close to the National Museum and Grand Palace, but also a tranquil option not far from the Khao San party zone. The very good Babble & Rum café has riverview garden seating, and there's a bar, a pool and a fitness centre.

Royal Hotel $$ *Ratchadamnoen Klang Road; tel: 0-2222 9111*. Bangkok's third-oldest hotel is a bit dated, but it stands within walking distance of Wat Phra Kaew and Wat Pho. Rooms in the old wing are larger than those in the new wing. There's a pleasant pool and a Chinese restaurant.

The Siam $$$$$ *3/2 Khao Road; tel: 0 2206 6999; www.thesiamhotel. com*. The Siam, which hugs the river beside the Krung Thon Bridge, is like a mini museum with antiques and artworks lining the public areas. The luxurious Art Deco rooms also have nods to historic Siam, and each comes with a personal butler and free wifi. Some buildings are old wooden houses brought from Ayutthaya by Jim Thompson.

Viengtai Hotel $$ *42 Rambutri Road; tel: 0 2280 5434; www.vieng tai.co.th*. Although dated in design, art and furnishings, the venerable Viengtai makes a more peaceful retreat than the hustle and bustle of Khao San Road close by. Friendly and efficient staff. Good travel agency and a swimming pool.

CENTRAL BANGKOK

A-One Inn $ *25/13–15 Soi Kasemsan 1, Rama I Road; tel: 0-2215 3029; www.aoneinn.com*. Very basic rooms, but this is a good location at this price, close to Siam Square shops, the Skytrain and several sites. The rooms do have satellite TV and air conditioning and there's an internet café with wi-fi, and a laundry service. It's a popular spot, but if it's full this street has other similar options.

InterContinental Bangkok $$$$ *973 Ploenchit Road; tel: 0-2656 0444; www.ichotelsgroup.com*. This is a good location, linked to Chidom Skytrain station and close to several shopping malls. The rooms are spacious and have internet access and CD players. The rooftop swimming pool has good views, and there are several good restaurants, including the Italian Grossi.

Four Seasons Bangkok $$$$ *155 Ratchadamri Road; tel: 0-2250 1000;* www.fourseasons.com. This world-class hotel is tastefully decorated with traditional and modern Thai art, including a striking temple-inspired mural over the massive lobby staircase. The trappings extend to the rooms, with teak and Thai silks dominating, and it has some of the best hotel dining in Bangkok. Located close to Rajadamri BTS station.

Grand Hyatt Erawan $$$$ *494 Ratchadamri Road; tel: 0-2254 1234;* www.bangkok.hyatt.com. Grandly executed neoclassical Thai architecture and a large collection of Thai modern art are the hallmarks here. Some rooms overlook the grassy turf of the Bangkok Royal Sports Club race track while most face adjacent buildings. The rooftop i.sawan residential spa offers a huge fitness centre, a swimming pool, and treatments that draw from traditional Thai medicine as well as modern spa technology.

Siam@Siam $$$ *865 Phra Rama I Road; tel: 0-2217 3000;* www.siamatsiam.com. A bright and contemporary hotel on the 14th–25th floors of a skyscaper. It features industrial design elements such as polished concrete and railway sleepers, as well as lots of wood and some splashes of colour. The rooms have superb views over the city centre and the National Stadium. The hotel features an excellent spa, a bar and good restaurants.

Siam Kempinski $$$$ *991/9 Rama I Road; tel: 0-2162 9000;* www.kempinski.com. Decked out with a grand interior, the Kempinski is well situated behind Siam Paragon mall for downtown shopping. The rooms have flat screen TVs, iPod connectivity, broadband internet and garden views, where there's a handsome pool. The modern Thai restaurant Sra Bua, a branch of Copenhagen's Michelin-starred Kiin Kiin, is well worth a visit.

SILOM AND BANGRAK

Baan Saladaeng 69/2 $$ *Saladaeng Soi 3; tel: 0-2636 3038;* www.baansaladaeng.com. Room names like Neo Siam, Moroccan Suite and Pop Art Mania mark out the funky approach at this tasteful budget operation. Each has aircon, TV and wireless internet, and there's a small coffee bar on site. Transport, restaurants and nightlife are just a short walk away.

Dusit Thani $$$ *946 Thanon Rama IV; tel: 0-2200 9999; www.dusit. com.* Opposite Lumpini Park, close Patpong's nightlife, and beside MRT and Skytrain stations, it's hard to find a better location to stay. The pick of 13 bars and restaurants is the modern Thai menu launched at Benjarong in 2014.

Mandarin Oriental $$$$$ *48 Soi Oriental, Charoen Krung Road; tel: 0-2659 9000; www.mandarinoriental.com/bangkok.* At the world famous Oriental, you can stay in the original building, which has hosted literary figures such as Joseph Conrad and Somerset Maugham, and is now known as the Author's Wing, or in one of two medium-rise wings. The hotel's personalised service is legendary, and there are several good restaurants, a jazz bar and an adjacent Express Boat pier.

Pullman Bangkok Hotel G $$$ *188 Silom Road; tel: 0-2238 1991; www.pullmanhotels.com.* This 38-storey hotel has chic, modern looking rooms with floor to ceiling windows overlooking the city. Good views, too, from Scarlett Wine Bar & Restaurant, on the 37th-floor; at ground level, 25 Degrees is a stylish burger joint. Chong Nonsi Skytrain station is a five-minute walk.

La Résidence $$ *173/8–9 Surawong Road; tel: 0-2233 3301; www. laresidencebangkok.com.* A boutique hotel with just 26 rooms in a very central location. Some rooms are very tiny but good value, others are more spacious, but all have spic and span bathrooms and a homely atmosphere. Very friendly staff.

Sukhothai $$$$ *13/3 South Sathon Road; tel: 0-2287 0222; www.suk hothai.com.* Architecturally the Sukhothai's tribute to postmodern Thai art echoes ancient Buddhist temple architecture with colonnaded exterior corridors and courtyard lily ponds punctuated by *stupas* and Buddha images. Teak-floored rooms are capacious and outfitted with amenities that will satisfy leisure and business travellers alike. The Celadon is one of Bangkok's top hotel-based Thai dining experiences and La Scala serves excellent Italian.

Take a Nap $ *920–6 Rama 4 Road; tel: 0-2637 0015; www.takeanap hotel.com.* Take a Nap has basic but attractive rooms, each with an artistic theme, such as Japanese waves, Pop Art, and the child-like Happy Forest, painted on the wall. There is air conditioning and a few TV stations available, but no fridges or wardrobes. It is close to the Patpong night market and just a five-minute walk to Skytrain and subway stations.

W Bangkok $$$$ *106 North Sathorn Road; tel: 0-2344 4000; www.w hotels.com.* The Bangkok flagship of the luxury modern W chain is next to Chong Nonsi skytrain station, in the middle of this fast developing business district. Purple, silver and black in the palette and a pool with underwater lighting and speakers illustrate its pitch at a younger market. Rooms have iPad docking to link with TV screens. A casual all-day restaurant serves international food.

SUKHUMVIT ROAD

Atlanta $ *78 Soi 2 (Soi Phasak), Sukhumvit Road; tel: 0-2252 6069; www.theatlantahotelbangkok.com.* Opened in the 1950s as the private Atlanta Rooms and suites at this atmospheric 1950s classic come in several size, price and quality ranges. Although only a stone's throw from the Nana red-light district, the Atlanta enforces a strict policy barring the sex trade from the premises. It has a Thai restaurant, and a period-perfect lobby and tropical-landscaped pool that turn up frequently in locally produced films and TV dramas.

Emporium Suites $$$ *622 Sukhumvit Soi 24; tel: 0-2664 9999; www. emporiumsuites.com.* This is a smart serviced apartment option with accommodation including studios and several sizes of suite up to 3-bedrooms All have wifi, flat screen TVs and cooking facilities. It sits above the Emporium shopping mall, and is connected to the Phrom Phong Skytrain Station. Some rooms have views of the adjacent Benjasiri Park.

The Eugenia $$$$ *267 Sukhumvit Soi 31; tel: 0-2259 9011; www. theeugenia.com.* This very cute hotel has 19th-century colonial-style decor in details like four-poster beds, antique furniture and accessories. There's an international restaurant, a spa and a free tuk tuk service to the nearest Skytrain station, and the style continues with city tours and airport transfers conducted in vintage Jaguars and Mercedes.

The Landmark $$$ *138 Sukhumvit Road; tel: 0-2254 0404; www.landmarkbangkok.com.* Located right on Sukhumvit Road, the Landmark offers easy access to Nana skytrain station and all the local bars and clubs. It has a good range of rooms and the quality top floor steak restaurant overlooking the city is the best of several food outlets.

JW Marriott $$$$ *4 Sukhumvit Road at Soi 2; tel: 0 2656 7700; www.jwmarriott.com.* This classy hotel is a top choice for both tourists and business travellers for its comfortably sleek lobby lounge, well-decorated rooms, state-of-the-art fitness centre and convenient location near the Nana BTS station. Tsu-Nami, a Japanese restaurant on the bottom floor, and The New York Steakhouse both serve top quality food.

Seven $$$ *3/15 Soi 31, Sukhumvit Road; tel: 0-2662 0951; www.sleepatseven.com.* Seven has six rooms and a communal lounge/bar/gallery space, each decorated in a different colour, inspired by the deep-rooted Thai belief that each day of the week has its own colour, reflecting a specific god. The contemporary Thai feel attracts a young, trendy crowd. Rooms are well equipped and come with free mobile phones.

Sheraton Grande Sukhumvit $$$$ *250 Sukhumvit Road; tel: 0-2649 8888; www.sheratongrandesukhumvit.com.* With a skywalk connection to skytrain and metro stations, you can be enroute from here within minutes, which is a big plus in Bangkok. It also has spacious rooms, a beautifully landscaped pool and an excellent spa. The Thai and Italian restaurants are both good, there's a lounge-bar-cum-nightclub and a very good jazz band in the Living Room.

Suk11 Hostel $ *1/33 Sukhumvit Soi 11; tel: 0-2253 5927; www.suk11.com.* The rooms have no TV or fridge, but this Thai-style guesthouse, with lots of wood and rustic decor, is on one of the city's liveliest downtown streets. There's internet access and cooking classes available, and it's a short walk from the Skytrain.

INDEX

Berlitz pocket guide

Bangkok

Third Edition 2015

Written by Joe Cummings
Updated by Howard Richardson
Edited by Sarah Clark
Picture Editor: Tom Smyth
Head of Production: Rebeka Davies

Photography credits: 123RF 3T, 4ML, 22, 48,
53, 59, 61, 73, 76, 98; Bigstock 58; Dreamstime
55, 69, 78; Frances Dorai/Apa Publications
2ML, 47; Hans Fonk 3M, 62, 63; iStock 2TC,
2/3M, 70, 81; John Ishii/Apa Publications 14;
Luca Tettoni 17; Mandarin Oriental 4TL; Nikt
Wong/Apa Publications 34; Peter Stuckings/
Apa Publications 1, 2TL, 2MC, 3TC, 2/3M, 2/3M,
4ML, 4MR, 4TL, 4/5M, 5MC, 4/5T, 5TC, 6TL,
6ML, 6ML, 7MC, 7MC, 7TC, 8, 10, 11, 12, 15, 18,
24, 26, 29, 30, 31, 32, 34/35, 36/37, 38, 39, 41, 42,
44/45, 50, 52, 54, 56, 65, 66, 66/67, 72, 74, 76/77,
82, 85, 86, 89, 91, 92, 96/97, 101, 103, 104, 106;
Piya Rangsit 20; Q Bar 95

Cover picture: AWL Images

Printed in China by CTPS

Berlitz Trademark Reg. U.S. Patent Office
and other countries. Marca Registrada.
Used under licence from the Berlitz
Investment Corporation

Every effort has been made to provide
accurate information in this publication,
but changes are inevitable. The publisher
cannot be responsible for any resulting
loss, inconvenience or injury.

Contact us

At Berlitz we strive to keep our guides as
accurate and up to date as possible, but if you
find anything that has changed, or if you have
any suggestions on ways to improve this guide,
then we would be delighted to hear from you.

Berlitz Publishing, PO Box 7910,
London SE1 1WE, England.
email: berlitz@apaguide.co.uk
www.insightguides.com/berlitz